THE EUROPEAN CONQUEST OF NORTH AMERICA

WORLD HISTORY LIBRARY

THE EUROPEAN CONQUEST OF NORTH AMERICA

CONSTANCE JONES

Facts On File®

AN INFOBASE HOLDINGS COMPANY

On the cover: detail from *The Exploits of Sun Boy*, 1885–90, pencil, colored pencil, ink, and commercial paint on muslin, done by Silverhorn (Haungooah) 1861–c.1941, Kiowa. In this painting, Silverhorn depicts scenes from the life of the Kiowa warrior Sun Boy in a style known as ledger style. The top two scenes show incidents with the U.S. Army that probably occurred in the 1860s. The bottom scene shows an 1870s incident with Texas Rangers.

The European Conquest of North America

Copyright © 1995 by Constance Jones

Facts On File, Inc.
460 Park Avenue South
New York NY 10016

Library of Congress Cataloging-in-Publication Data

Jones, Constance, 1961–
    The European conquest of North America / by Constance Jones.
        p.   cm. — (World history library)
    Includes bibliographical references and index.
    ISBN 0-8160-3041-3
        1. Indians of North America—History.   2. North America–History.
I. Title. II. Series.
E77.J75 1995   94-12470
970.01—dc20

Facts On File books are available at special discounts when purchased in bulk quantities for businesses, associations, institutions or sales promotions. Please call our Special Sales Department in New York at 212/683-2244 or 800/322-8755.

Text design by Donna Sinisgalli
Cover design by Amy Gonzalez
Maps by Dale Williams

Printed in the United States of America

MP FOF 10 9 8 7 6 5 4 3 2 1

This book is printed on acid-free paper.

CONTENTS

THE EUROPEAN CONQUEST OF NORTH AMERICA

THE FIRST NORTH AMERICANS

The Americas were isolated almost completely from the rest of the world before Italian explorer Christopher Columbus reached the islands of the Caribbean Sea in 1492. Made up of the two continents of the earth's Western Hemisphere—North America and South America—including the Caribbean islands, the landmass stretches almost from pole to pole, forming the western boundary of the Atlantic Ocean. Like a giant roadblock to anyone sailing west from Europe, the continents kept Columbus from his intended destination, the Indies (China, Japan, Indonesia, India, and neighboring lands).

Although America consists of two continents, geographers and scholars often divide it into three regions. The first is the entire continent of South America, from present-day Colombia in the northwest to Cape Horn at the southernmost tip of Chile. The second region, known as Central America or Middle America, actually contains the southern reaches of North America, from the modern United States–

**Indian Tribes of North America
Before the Arrival of Columbus**

Mexico border in the north to the isthmus of Panama in the south. This area also encompasses the Caribbean islands and the Bahamas. Made up of present-day Canada and the United States, the third region is what most people now refer to as North America.

The European conquest of all three regions represented an event of profound importance in world history. Because the whole story is so sweeping and complex, this book will deal only with the conquest of North America. It was there that the Europeans most successfully transplanted their own culture to foreign soil. Although colonization and settlement did not originally figure greatly in Europe's plans for America, white migration ultimately became key to the global balance of economic and political power. As European empires expanded westward across the Atlantic, America came to be known as the New World. The name suggested an unclaimed territory free for the taking, a place created by God for the benefit of white, Christian Europe.

But up to 12 million people already lived there, in every region from the frozen tundra to subtropical wetlands, from endlessly flat prairies to towering mountain ranges. Hundreds of cultures flourished in harmony with the diverse geography and climate of a land that covered about 7.5 million square miles (about 12 million square kilometers). Verdant forests, fertile plains, arid deserts, teeming marshes, rainy coastlands, wind-swept plateaus, and many other environments supported peoples superbly adapted to survival in their chosen home. Some groups had lived in the same territory for thousands of years, others had migrated from place to place for centuries. Ancient similarities of language, technology, and belief linked the peoples of North America together, but a tremendous range of variations distinguished one group from another. The Seminole of Florida, the Inuit of the Arctic, the Mohawk of the Northeast woodlands, and the Hopi of the Southwest differed physically, socially, and economically from each other and from the many other cultures that thrived in North America in 1492.

North America may have represented a New World to the Europeans who arrived in the 15th century, but people had inhabited the continent for millennia. Archaeologists have determined that *Homo sapiens* did not evolve from earlier hominids in the Western Hemisphere; rather, fully evolved humans migrated there starting as long as 35,000 years ago. They came during the Ice Age, when sea levels dropped because ocean waters froze into icepack glaciers. The lowered seas exposed a wide land bridge that spanned the Bering Strait between present-day Siberia and Alaska. In search of mammoths, mastodons, and other Ice Age game, nomadic hunters ventured across the land bridge from Asia to America. Over the years, the bridge was submerged for centuries at a time, temporarily halting the migration before resurfacing again. It disappeared for good around 10,000 years ago, cutting the people of America off from the rest of the world.

Groups of people arriving at different times spread southward and eastward via different routes, gradually populating the entire continent. This process took a very long time. Sometimes, as people migrated, glaciers sealed the way behind them, isolating earlier arrivals from later immigrants. In isolation, ancient cultures developed independently, adapting to the varying demands of the environment. Groups in harsher climates devised ingenious ways to survive, generally living as nomadic hunters and gatherers. In more hospitable zones, ancient North Americans moved from hunting, fishing, and gathering nuts and berries to agriculture, which allowed groups to settle permanently in one place and their populations to grow.

The many cultures scattered across North America met different natural challenges that caused each group to develop along different lines. But all shared a need to establish a niche in the order of nature, to live off the bounty of the land. As a result, the vastly diverse peoples had certain features in common. Most had an array of tools and implements ranging from spears, bows and arrows, and knives to canoes, baskets, and ceramic pottery. The majority were relatively peaceful, staging only occasional raids on their neighbors rather than waging protracted wars. Generally farming maize (corn), squash, beans, and potatoes, agricultural peoples also raised a number of regional crops. Many cultures based their social organization around clans, groups of people with a common ancestor. Whatever its social structure, each people held its territory in common for the use of all members.

Harboring deep respect for the earth and all its creatures, the first North Americans developed religions, myths, and legends centered on faith in supernatural forces that linked people with all living things. Humanity was viewed as the equal—not the master—of animals and plants, which had their own spirits. The earth was often described as a mother to be cherished and thanked for providing the means of survival. A hunter's or farmer's success depended on his or her alignment with natural forces. Of course, some practices harmed the environment, but populations were rarely large enough to cause widespread or lasting damage. Survival and prosperity flowed not from struggle and achievement but from a respectful relationship with nature. This philosophy would eventually come into direct conflict with the beliefs and desires of the European conquerors. Every indigenous North American culture, wherever it lived, would suffer the consequences of Europe's imperial ambitions.

THE ARCTIC AND SUBARCTIC

In the northernmost reaches of America, a number of resourceful peoples extracted a surprisingly abundant living from the frozen earth. Much of the most remote area, located above the Arctic Circle and known as the Arctic, is covered by ice year-round, while brushy tundra grows where the snow melts in summer. Two cultures made their home in the Arctic and continue to do so today: the Inuit and the Aleut. Their broad faces, narrow eyes, and short, plump physiques set them firmly apart from other indigenous Americans. Some archaeologists believe they migrated later than more southerly groups, arriving by sea around 3000 B.C. No matter what their origins, the Inuit lived a unique life. The Aleut, who inhabited a chain of islands to the southwest of Alaska, had much in common with them, but also shared many traits with the peoples of the Pacific Northwest Coast.

A nomadic hunting people with almost no opportunity for agriculture, the Inuit relied on seals, whales, walrus, fish, and shellfish in the winters and added caribou and birds to their diet in the summers. Europeans called them Eskimo, a derogatory term meaning "eaters of raw meat," which originated with other indigenous groups. The animals the Inuit caught provided flesh for food; skins and fur for clothing, tents, and kayaks; fat for oil lamps; and bone, horn, and ivory for tools, fishing gear, and household items. Skilled carvers of ivory and bone, the Inuit etched intricate designs into their implements. Living in small, widely dispersed family units, they took shelter in tents and in wood, wood-and-sod, and sod-and-stone houses. The domed snow house known as the igloo was used rarely on the Alaskan peninsula and more often in the Arctic portion of present-day Canada. The Inuit moved about in search of game, using sleds drawn by domesticated dogs. Harpoons, ice picks, studded boots, and sun goggles helped them snare their quarry. Each winter, groups of families gathered for festivals of dancing, storytelling, singing contests, and gymnastics.

To the south of the Inuit, in the region between the Arctic and the Great Lakes, lived the peoples of the Subarctic. The eastern portion of their homeland was rugged and mountainous, while the western portion featured gentle hills, numerous lakes and rivers, and marshy bogs. Vegetation was limited to tundra in the north, but farther south the land was covered by evergreen forests and grassy meadows. Sparsely populated, the Subarctic supported two broad groups of people: the Athapascan-speaking peoples west of Hudson Bay, such as the Yellowknife, Ingalik, and Tagish, and the Algonquian-speaking peoples east of the bay, such as the Naskapi and the Cree. A small group called the Beothuk had their own language. These groups followed essentially the same way of life, relying on hunting, fishing, and foraging rather than on agriculture.

Independent family groups led a nomadic life in search of moose, caribou, musk oxen, buffalo, bear, elk, and smaller game, taking fish and wild fowl along the way. Traveling by canoe, toboggan, and snowshoe, they hunted with bows and arrows as well as snares, spears, and nets. Unable to cultivate food so far north, they gathered roots and berries to supplement their diet. They lived in a variety of temporary dwellings, from tipis and wigwams to wooden and earthen houses. Implements of wood, stone, and horn were used to craft clothing and household items of hide, fur, and fiber. At times, the Subarctic peoples decorated themselves with jewelry, face paint, and tattoos that reflected their spiritual beliefs. More warlike than their northern neighbors, the people of the Subarctic carried an array of clubs, lances, and shields.

THE PACIFIC NORTHWEST COAST

Based on a narrow strip of Pacific Ocean coastline that stretches as far north as Alaska and as far south as northern California, the peoples of the Pacific Northwest Coast enjoyed an unusually prosperous and leisurely life before Europeans arrived. They owed their comfort to an exceptionally livable environment, which offered mild temperatures and plentiful rainfall year-round. Between the Cascade Range and the sea, wild game and edible plant life abounded along rivers and lakes in lush forest land. The sea and rivers provided a seemingly inexhaustible supply of salmon, whales, and other creatures to anyone with a canoe. So generous was the land of the Pacific Northwest that the people there had no need either to work farms or to wander as nomadic hunters. Nature brought everything to them.

In this bountiful home, the Northwest Coast people could accumulate the wealth necessary to support complex and stable cultures. About 50 distinct groups inhabited the region, including the Tlingit, Kwakiutl, Coastal Salish, Chinook, Yurok, and Tolowa. They lived in large, permanent towns that consisted of rows of roomy wooden houses with gabled roofs that repelled the frequent rain. Clothing and blankets of shredded cedar bark and animal fur kept them warm and dry, as did basket-woven rainhats. To enhance their appearance, the people often indulged in nose piercing, tattooing, and the flattening of infants' heads with cradleboards. The more northerly peoples of the Pacific Northwest enjoyed a higher standard of living than those to the south, but all the groups engaged in active trade.

Because they did not need to devote much time to survival, the Northwest Coast peoples spent their days pursuing other concerns, which included warfare with other groups to secure slaves. They also produced stunning visual arts and were among the world's great woodworkers. Artisans carved elaborate canoes up to 60 feet (18 meters) long as well as beautiful helmets, shields, masks, house posts, and door poles depicting their history and myths. From their woodworking tradition, during the 19th century, would come the so-called totem pole that whites still associate with all indigenous North Americans. Northwest Coast artforms celebrated the rich religious life their prosperity allowed. Powerful shamans and myriad secret societies performed ritual dances and ceremonies in honor of the many spirit beings that peopled the Northwest Coast cosmos.

With wealth came an obsession with property and prestige. Northwest Coast societies were stratified into different classes based on the status conferred by wealth. A person's wealth might consist of practical and decorative items, slaves, and nonmaterial things such as songs and heraldic crests. The people of the Pacific Northwest avidly sought these things for the stature they brought, a pursuit that evolved into a ritual known as the potlatch. To earn distinction, a host would invite friends and rivals to a potlatch, where he would destroy or give away valuable property to demonstrate how rich he was. While he burned baskets and blankets or gave away carved boxes and sheets of copper, he boasted about himself and insulted his rivals. Guests who hoped to maintain their own status would in turn have to host their own potlatches and try to outdo the first host. The more valuables a potlach host could dispose of, the more power he gained; the most lavish hosts could earn the rank of nobles. During the 19th century, the relentless competition would make the potlatches of the Northwest Coast peoples dizzyingly excessive.

EAST OF THE MISSISSIPPI

Between the Gulf of St. Lawrence and the Gulf of Mexico, the eastern portion of North America was home to dozens of cultures. These groups lived in wet coastal lowlands, lushly forested mountains and uplands (such as the Appalachian, Ozark, and Blue Ridge mountains), and fertile interior highlands. The climate ranged from very cold around the Great Lakes to tropical around the Mississippi River Delta, from foggy around Prince Edward Island and Nova Scotia to sunny on the Florida peninsula. Everywhere, game and vegetation were plentiful, providing a good life to the people.

When studying the first Americans, anthropologists generally divide eastern North America into the Northeast woodlands and the Southeast. In the Northeast woodlands, the many coastal peoples dependent on the sea included the Micmac, Penobscot, Massachuset, and Pequot to the north and the Delaware, Powhatan, Pamlico, and Catawba to the south. All of them fished the waters of the Atlantic and gathered shellfish along the shoreline; the seminomadic northern groups supplemented their diet by hunting and the more settled southern groups by farming. Inland, agriculture was the basis of life for groups such as the Huron, Iroquois, Ojibwa (Chippewa), Kickapoo, Shawnee, and Susquehanna (Conestoga). These farmers of maize, squash, beans, sunflowers, and tobacco also gathered berries, wild rice, and maple syrup. Many of them used the slash-and-burn farming technique to clear fresh plots of land each year.

The agricultural peoples of the Northeast lived in permanent villages protected by stockades, which enclosed rows of rectangular

A typical fortified Indian village in 16th-century Virginia. (Picture Collection, The Branch Libraries, The New York Public Library)

longhouses. Constructed of logs, or of pole frames covered with bark or hides, the longhouses featured barrel-shape roofs. The buildings could shelter dozens of people; some villages had as many as 3,000 residents. Although the villages were largely independent, most of the people had a strong tribal identity that linked them with other villages. Traders took goods from settlement to settlement, bringing along belts of seashell wampum as a kind of money. Within and among villages, community structure rested on clans. Some clans traced their descent through their mothers, and women held much of the political power in the group. Women selected the male representatives who sat on clan and tribal councils; they also served as priests and shamans alongside men.

The spiritual life of many Northeast peoples was quite complex, involving a belief in numerous spirits and participation in feasts and festivals at which they smoked ritual pipes of tobacco. Between 100 B.C. and A.D. 700, the peoples of the Ohio, Mississippi, and Illinois river valleys built large burial mounds that reflected a belief in the afterlife. The members of this Hopewell Culture buried beautiful artwork, such as basketry, jewelry, and pottery, with their dead. From artifacts found in the mounds, archaeologists have concluded that the Hopewell Culture was remarkably sophisticated.

Warfare was another prominent feature of Northeast woodland culture. Traveling in birchbark canoes and armed with bows and arrows, spears, and tomahawks, Northeast tribes frequently fought each other to expand or defend territory or to avenge intertribal insults. They battled fiercely, often brutally torturing their prisoners. Exhausted by war, the five Iroquois tribes—the Mohawk, Oneida, Onondaga, Cayuga, and Seneca—reached an agreement sometime between 1560 and 1570 and united into the League of Five Nations. (See box p. 11 .) When the Tuscarora moved north from the Carolinas in the early 18th century, they joined the organization, making it the League of Six Nations.

After the Hopewell Culture of the Northeast declined, the Southeast witnessed the rise of its own great Mississippian Culture starting in the eighth century. A highly structured society, it pursued intensive agriculture from farming villages that surrounded large, fortified ceremonial centers. The ceremonial centers included temple mounds probably used to worship a sun god. Archaeologists have found a wide variety of craft items, including exceptional pottery, in Mississippian sites. At its peak in the 16th century, the Mississippian Culture extended from the

THE EUROPEAN CONQUEST OF NORTH AMERICA

THE TREE OF THE GREAT PEACE

When the five warring Iroquois tribes along the southern coast of Lake Ontario called a truce in the 1560s, they formed the League of Five Nations under the leadership of Huron mystic Deganawida and Mohawk chief Hiawatha. The preamble of the Iroquois constitution underscores the importance of peace among the Mohawk, Oneida, Onondaga, Cayuga, and Seneca peoples:

> I am Deganawida and with the Five Nations' confederate lords I plant the Tree of the Great Peace. . . . I name the tree the Tree of the Great Long Leaves. Under the shade of this Tree of the Great Peace we spread the soft, white, feathery down of the globe thistle. . . . There shall you sit and watch the council fire of the Confederacy of the Five Nations.
>
> Roots have spread out from the Tree of the Great Peace . . . and the name of these roots is the Great White Roots of Peace. If any man of any nation outside of the Five Nations shall show a desire to obey the laws of the Great Peace . . . they may trace the roots to their source . . . and they shall be welcomed to take shelter beneath the Tree of the Long Leaves.
>
> The smoke of the confederate council fire shall ever ascend and shall pierce the sky so that all nations may discover the central council fire of the Great Peace.
>
> I, Deganawida, and the confederate lords now uproot the tallest pine tree and into the cavity thereby made we cast all weapons of war. Into the depths of the earth, down into the deep underneath currents of water flowing into unknown regions, we cast all weapons of strife. We bury them from sight forever and plant again the tree. Thus shall all Great Peace be established and hostilities shall no longer be known between the Five Nations but only peace to a united people.

lower Ohio River valley to present-day Louisiana and from the Florida peninsula to present-day Texas.

Before they moved, the Tuscarora lived in the Southeast region near another group of cultures. Like the Northeast woodland peoples, the Southeast peoples had a strong tribal affinity. From the Cherokee, Creek, and Seminole in the east to the Chickasaw, Choctaw, Tunica, and Caddo in the west, the many cultures shared an agricultural economy based on maize, beans, melons, and tobacco. Their large farming towns encompassed 100 or more dwellings each and were linked into strong confederacies that controlled wide areas of land. The stability of agricultural life allowed them to develop hierarchical societies, complex religions, and leisure-time games. Within their territory, members of each group traveled by dugout canoe and cane raft to hunt bear, deer, turkey, and other wild fowl, to fish, and to forage for nuts and berries.

THE PLAINS

Today, when people think of the old American West and the American Indian, they often think of wide-open grasslands and warriors on horseback. In fact, the indigenous people of the North American plains, popularized in novels and movies as warpainted buffalo hunters in feather bonnets and fringed buckskin, did not use horses until Europeans brought the animals with them from overseas. And only some of the cultures fit this stereotype of the Native American—the people of the dry western plains known as the Great Plains. To their east, on the more humid interior plains, the prairie peoples more often pursued agriculture. Taken together, the two plains regions stretch from the Mississippi River to the Rocky Mountains and from present-day Saskatchewan to Texas.

Cultures that called the interior plains home included the Osage, Missouri, Kansa, Omaha, Hidatsa, Pawnee, Wichita, and the various Sioux (Lakota) tribes. Their generally large, semipermanent settlements consisted of circular earth and mud lodges and plots of maize, squash, sunflowers, and beans. While women did most of the farming, men hunted small game. Especially among northern groups, who lived in walled towns, trade in furs and implements was an important component of the economy. North and south, the farther west the people lived, the drier the climate became and the less they relied on agriculture. Hunting and gathering were more important, and some villages sent bands of hunters out to the Great Plains in search of buffalo. More nomadic than the easternmost groups, these people resembled the inhabitants of the high plains in many ways. They lived in tipis (conical skin tents) and had many of the same warlike habits.

The nomadic hunters of the Great Plains relied almost entirely on the buffalo for survival. Such peoples as the Blackfoot, Crow, Cheyenne, Arapaho, Comanche, and Kiowa followed the vast herds to their favored hunting grounds in season. Traveling on foot, they used dogs to drag their possessions on travois, slings of hide supported by tipi poles. They set up seasonal tipi villages and hunted on foot with spears and bows and arrows; sometimes they drove herds of buffalo over cliffs. Using every part of the animal, they cooked fresh meat, dried meat into jerky, and made bone and horn utensils, buffalo robes, and leather tipi covers, clothing, and moccasins.

The Great Plains peoples' nomadic way of life allowed for little formal government: Each band had its own leader and council, but no chief oversaw an entire tribe. Without the guidance of any central authority, bands traded with each other, raided each other, and reached individual truces. Often preceded by war dances, raids were conducted to secure booty or earn honor for the warriors, who sometimes wore eagle feathers in their hair for strength and courage. The Blackfoot, Comanche, and Kiowa had a reputation as the fiercest warriors on the plains. During war or peacetime, members of a band or a tribe could communicate over long distances using smoke signals. Each year related bands gathered for enormous festivals at which dances and rituals were performed for the pleasure of the spirits. Secret male societies explored spiritual mysteries; men sought divine guidance through dreams, fasting, vision quests, and self-torture.

THE ROCKIES AND WESTWARD

Four cultural areas occupied North America west of the Great Plains: the Plateau between the Rocky Mountains and the Cascade Range, the Great Basin between the Rockies and the Sierra Nevada, California, and the Southwest. Each supported many peoples who had much in common with their neighbors but who differed greatly from groups in other areas.

On the Plateau, the northernmost region of the Far West, the well-watered mountains were covered with forests, lakes, and rivers. The local peoples, who included the Yakima, Spokan, Nez Percé, and Columbia, lived primarily by fishing salmon and did some hunting and foraging for roots and berries. Small, semipermanent settlements, each with its own leader, traded with each other. Through trade, many groups were influenced by the Pacific Northwest coastal peoples to the west; the basketry and dugout canoes of the Plateau reflect some of that influence. Although the Plateau peoples had little tribal cohesion, they occasionally banded together for hunting or defense against outsiders. The annual Winter Spirit dance brought many groups together to seek contact with their guardian spirits via shamans. In winter the people lived in round dwellings dug into hillsides and covered with earthen roofs; in summer they moved into domed pole structures draped with reed mats. Their lives were modest but comfortable.

By contrast, the peoples of the Great Basin to the south had a much harder lot. Among these groups were the Ute, Shoshone (Snake), Paiute, and others. Their home, which extended as far north as present-day Idaho and as far south as Arizona, was exceptionally arid. As a result, they roved constantly in small, widely scattered bands, hunting for antelope, rabbits, other small game, rodents, reptiles, and fish. Most often they survived on the brink of starvation by eating the roots, seeds, berries, and insects they found. Their constant struggle to feed themselves left little time or energy for waging war, refining crafts, devising religious systems, or building complex societies. Wandering bands consisted of family groups of 20 to 35 people; groups of several bands camped together in winter. Dressed in little more than sandals, they constructed wickiups—brush huts or lean-tos—for shelter.

Living an equally simple but far less austere life, the more than 100 California peoples enjoyed the blessings of a mild climate. The Shasta, Yokut, Chumash, and Cahuilla were only a few of the fishers, hunters, and gatherers for whom the acorn represented the main staple of an abundant diet. On foot, small and independent groups followed seasonal migration patterns within clearly defined territories. The warm and sunny weather required little or no clothing and only rudimentary

Ute Indians of the Great Basin in traditional dress. (Picture Collection, The Branch Libraries, The New York Public Library)

shelter, which they built in conical or domed form of brush, bark, and earth. Because they spent little energy on survival, they managed to develop crafts such as basketry of the highest quality. But the peoples of California spent most of their leisure time in social and spiritual pursuits. Their clan-based culture included a basic legal system in which injured or offended parties received payment from those who wronged them. Filled with festivals, games, initiation rites, dances, songs, and ceremonial societies, their religious life was rich. In the north, the Pacific Northwest Coast cultures influenced some groups; in the south, the influence came from the peoples of the Southwest.

The indigenous peoples of the Southwest, who lived in an area that encompasses present-day Arizona and parts of New Mexico, Utah, Colorado, and Texas, had a long and colorful history. Starting in the first century A.D., the majestic Anasazi culture thrived in the area, advancing agriculture, village life, and ceramics to high levels of sophistication. About A.D. 700 the Pueblo Culture began to supplant the Anasazi, introducing large settlements of multifamily pueblo dwellings made of mud. The most famous Pueblo sites are Mesa Verde, a pueblo built into a cliff cave in southwestern Colorado, and Chaco Canyon, a large settlement in northwest New Mexico, both constructed between 1100 and 1300. Around 1450, for reasons that remain mysterious, the Pueblo peoples abandoned many of their towns, including Mesa Verde and Chaco Canyon.

Heirs to the Anasazi and Pueblo traditions, the people who inhabited the Southwest when Europeans arrived included the Havasupai, Mojave, Yuma, Navajo, Hopi, and Zuñi. Some of them lived in pueblos in close-knit communities where the needs of the group superseded the needs of the individual. They valued conformity to social norms, which were determined most often by powerful religious societies. Centered around kivas, ceremonial structures open only to men, religious activity focused on spirits known as kachinas. Costumed, mask-wearing priests impersonated the kachinas and distributed dolls representing the spirits in long, myth-filled rituals. One goal of their religion was a good harvest. The main crop, maize, was supplemented by squash, beans, cotton, tobacco, and gourds. While the men farmed, the women made elegant baskets and pottery, cooked the food, and built the pueblos.

The Pueblo peoples sometimes fell prey to assaults by nomadic Apache raiders who roamed between the Great Plains and the Southwest. As the Apache passed through their territory, the Navajo picked up some of their customs. Surviving mostly as hunters and gatherers, the Navajo also did some farming. They learned how to make beautiful jewelry as well as clothing of animal skins and plant fibers. Based in villages of hogans (low, domed shelters constructed of logs and mud), independent bands kept watch over their territory. Organized into clans, they traced their ancestry matrilineally—that is, through their mothers' families. At times, bands of the same clan came together to hunt or to conduct religious rituals. The purpose of Navajo religious life was to achieve harmony with the universe.

For many of the indigenous peoples of North America, the quality of life plummeted after Europeans arrived. With disastrous results for the first Americans, European disease and encroachment decimated their numbers throughout the continent after 1492. Many individuals—and some entire groups—died of diseases such as smallpox, measles, and typhus, or were killed by whites who wanted their land. The survivors were forced into smaller, inferior territories as white settlement advanced. In only a few short centuries, indigenous North Americans lost their ancestral homelands and much of their cultural heritage to the European conquest. Today fewer than 3 million Native Americans live in the United States and Canada.

CHAPTER ONE NOTE

p. 11   "I am Deganawida . . ." Quoted in William N. Fenton, ed. *Parker on the Iroquois* (Syracuse, NY: Syracuse University Press, 1968), pp. 8–9.

EUROPE'S
TASTE FOR
EMPIRE

Before the age of European exploration and expansion, the peoples of Asia and the Middle East dominated world culture. Europe languished in the Dark Ages, hobbled by fragmented political systems and a depressed economy. The dominance of strict religious beliefs slowed development of European arts, scholarly pursuits, and technology. But a shift in the state of European affairs began slowly in the 14th century and gathered speed and scope in the phenomenon known as the Renaissance. This far-reaching cultural movement forever changed every aspect of European life. Small principalities and kingdoms united into powerful nations. Feudalism, a rigidly stratified political, economic, and social structure, gave way to new forms of commerce that spurred the rise of prosperous towns. The Protestant Reformation and Catholic Counter-Reformation liberalized religion, paving the way for greater intellectual and artistic freedom.

During the Renaissance, European interest in world exploration and conquest blossomed. The two centuries preceding Columbus's first voyage saw the rediscovery of ancient Greek and Roman scholarship and a revival of secular education. Johannes Gutenberg's invention of movable type around 1440 revolutionized printing methods, permitting a wider and more rapid spread of information. As learning increased, so did curiosity about the world beyond European borders. At the same time, the new nation-states grew in strength and competed with each other for power, prestige, and glory. They now had the means to finance foreign expeditions that promised to add wealth to their treasuries and land to their territories. Another motivation for venturing abroad was the desire to establish Christianity in place of other religions throughout the world. Among the nations that reached out to every corner of the earth, Spain, England, the Netherlands, France, Sweden, and Russia sent ships to North America. Because of the global impact it would ultimately have, the start of European exploration and expansion in the 15th century marked the dawn of a new era of history.

A WORLD BEYOND

Since ancient times, Europeans had entertained the possibility that an unknown land lay over the sea to the west. In *Medea,* the Roman philosopher Seneca predicted that "An age will come after many years when the Ocean will loose the chain of things, and a huge land lie revealed." The Romans believed in the *Insulae Fortunatae,* or Happy Isles, said to lie across the western ocean. There, according to legend, life was perfectly good and bounteous; some believed the islands served as a way-station for the dead on their way to the afterlife. St. Brendan, an Irish friar, was said to have led a group of monks to several mysterious Atlantic islands in the sixth century.

More recently, speculation about early American contact with the rest of the world has focused on possible "drift voyages" to and from the continents. Drift voyages, carried out without sophisticated navigational equipment, take boats wherever the ocean currents lead. Proponents of the drift voyage theory have claimed that in ancient times, people may have arrived on North American shores from such faraway places as Japan, Egypt, Libya, Ireland, Phoenicia, and Europe's Pyrenees Mountains.

Modern experts, however, have turned up archaeological evidence of only one instance of European contact with the New World before

Columbus. This evidence comes from L'Anse aux Meadows in present-day Newfoundland, Canada, where Norse Vikings established a short-lived fishing colony in the 11th century. Norse sagas tell of a Viking named Biarni Heriulfson, who sailed from Iceland in 986 and reached Baffin Island, off the coast of Labrador. Following the same route, Leif Eriksson arrived in Newfoundland, which he called Vinland, in 1000. Thorfinn Karlsefni led 160 Norse colonists to Vinland in 1003. There they lived until 1015, when indigenous people evicted them from the prized fishing grounds. The Norse experience in North America remained all but unknown to the rest of Europe until the 19th century, so it had no impact on the exploration and expansion of the Renaissance.

European interest in sailing west in search of unknown lands grew steadily during the 15th century. Because the learned people of the time knew the earth was round, some geographers proposed that it was possible to reach the eastern lands known as the Indies by sailing west across the Atlantic. Much debate surrounded the question of exactly how many days such a trip might take, but most geographers felt sure the journey would be impossibly long. Some experts, however, remained certain Asia did not lay too far over the sea from Europe. The Portuguese discovery of the Azores in 1432 raised European hopes that Asia was within reach. Columbus, a master mariner, numbered among the believers and dreamed of making the trip decades before he finally set sail. One of those who agreed with his point of view was Italian geographer Pablo Toscanelli, who told him in 1474, "The voyage you wish to undertake is not as difficult as people think; on the contrary, the ship's course is certain. . . ."

GOLD, SPICES, AND JEWELS

European interest in exploring the world was, of course, more than intellectual. Economics featured prominently in the dreams and plans of would-be adventurers. The growth of Europe's population, which was also growing more prosperous, swelled demand for imported goods. At the same time, Europe was producing more goods than ever before, and it required both sources of raw materials and expanded markets in which to sell its exports. Anyone who could fill the gap through trade was bound to turn a profit.

TOOLS OF THE TRADE

Advances in the technology of navigation, cartography, and boat-building during the Renaissance allowed seafaring Europeans to sail out of sight of land for ever longer voyages. The

A 16th-century caravel, on whose quarterdeck a navigator uses an astrolabe. (Picture Collection, The Branch Libraries, The New York Public Library)

During the Renaissance, an economic system known as mercantilism gained ascendancy in Europe. In mercantilism, the economy was driven by the profit motive instead of the old patterns of feudalism. The focus on earning money—among laborers, their employers, and national governments—increased the importance of gold and silver in the European economy. More than ever before, the wealth of nations came to depend on the amount of these metals in their treasuries. Gold and silver gave Europe access to highly desirable Asian exports, such simple magnet, in the form of the compass, revolutionized ocean travel. Mariners had known the compass since the 12th century, when it came to Europe from China, but it was not until the 15th century that they discovered its full potential. Finding new uses for tools used by astronomers, they also learned new ways of navigating by the stars. The astrolabe, the quadrant, and the cross-staff allowed sailors to chart their latitude from their position relative to the sun and Polaris (the North Star). From there it was only a short step to improved charts that mapped the seas in greater detail.

Among the first to employ the new navigational tools, the Portuguese made another original and invaluable contribution to ocean travel. As they ventured far from home down the African coast, they developed a sturdier, more seaworthy type of sailing ship than Europe had ever seen before. The caravel, equipped with more masts, improved rigging, and large, square sails, was faster and easier to maneuver than the ships previously available to European mariners. It could withstand rough weather and stay at sea as long as provisions held out. During their African explorations, the Portuguese in their caravels engaged in increasingly extended expeditions that accustomed European sailors to the idea of lengthy voyages. Before long, shipbuilders in other countries produced their own versions of the caravel.

as spices, medicines, perfumes, gems, rugs, and silk. But Europe boasted no significant gold or silver mines. It could obtain the precious metals only through trade with or conquest of others. To sustain their treasuries, the nations of Europe needed to find new markets for their exports, which included wine, glassware, and wool.

The Portuguese sought new markets for their exports in Africa, where they made contact with gold-rich cultures. They also pressed down the continent's Atlantic coast in search of a direct water route to the Indies. Such a route could boost profits from foreign trade by making it more efficient. Previously, travel between Europe and Asia had involved a combination of water and overland transportation across the many countries of the Middle East. At each step of the journey, local authorities levied taxes on goods, shippers charged fees to move them, and intermediary traders took their own profits. The long and costly process meant European merchants made less money than they could if they dealt directly with their Asian counterparts.

European demand for Asian merchandise continued to grow. The unpleasant realities of daily life before refrigeration and indoor plumbing were compounded in burgeoning towns and cities. Garbage and sewage were dumped in the streets, people seldom bathed, and food spoiled quickly. To combat the foul odors that permeated the air, Europeans sought the perfumes and oils produced in the East. To preserve food and disguise the flavor of meat and produce past its prime, they sought Asian spices. After Venetian explorer Marco Polo traveled to the Far East and published his impressions at the end of the 13th century, European interest in Asia exploded. Polo's accounts of the region's immense wealth made Europeans more eager than ever to expand trade with the Indies. Alongside government-sponsored efforts, private investors formed corporations to finance for-profit exploration.

FOR GOD AND COUNTRY

As Christians, most European traders disliked traveling the old caravan routes, which ran through the Muslim-dominated Middle East. These routes were disrupted during the Crusades of the 11th through 13th centuries, when European military campaigns attempted to wrest control of the Holy Land from the "infidels."

The Crusades were an expression of Christian Europe's appetite for religious conquest. At the start of the Renaissance, all Christians in western Europe practiced Roman Catholicism. One imperative of their church was to convert all the world's nonbelievers to Catholicism, by force if necessary. In the process, the church claimed the wealth of the vanquished; for some church leaders greed replaced fervor as the reason for conquest. Likewise, European rulers seeking to expand the scope of their power and to add wealth to their coffers could justify imperialism on religious grounds. As the Crusaders tried but failed to overpower the Muslim peoples of the Middle East, a frustrated, Catholic Europe began to look elsewhere for victory.

In Portugal and Spain, Catholic rulers faced the "infidel" enemy on their own soil. North African Moors invaded the Iberian peninsula in the eighth century and conquered the local peoples, establishing Islam and dominating the culture. Over the next several centuries, the Spanish and Portuguese fought the Muslim intruders and gradually forced them out, evicting the last of them from the Spanish province of Granada in 1492. The long struggle produced strong monarchies in both countries and a powerful military capable of ambitious operations.

Europe's sense of holy mission gained urgency after the Protestant Reformation, which divided Christian Europe into two camps early in the 16th century. Spearheaded by a German monk named Martin Luther and John Calvin, a French expatriate living in Switzerland, movements to reform the Catholic church instead produced several new Christian sects. England, the Netherlands, and most of the other countries of northern Europe adopted various forms of Protestantism, while Spain, France, and the rest of southern Europe remained Catholic.

Like Catholics, Protestants wanted to convert nonbelievers to their "true" religion. The missionary impulse placed Catholic and Protestant nations in competition with each other for international spiritual influence. When Columbus reported finding land across the Atlantic, Europeans rushed to claim the western territories for their respective churches.

Of course, the rivalry between European states predated the Protestant Reformation. Cultural pride as well as economic and political ambition had always divided Europe. During the Renaissance, the formation of large, centralized nation-states created a potent new form of nationalism. In many countries, this patriotism was for the first time backed up by a powerful ruler, a professional army, and a large economy. Exploration and expansion became a national goal. Europeans wanted more land, not just for its practical and economic value, but as a point of national prestige.

Until the Renaissance, few central monarchs had much power over the aristocracy, who controlled the economy and often formed their own armies. Nation-states began to form only when the strength of the nobility faded. Constant warfare between nobles and their role in the Crusades killed many of them and sapped their wealth. Kings and queens took greater control of national economic and political life, building states much richer and mightier than the small feudal fragments. Firearms technology, which leapt forward with the introduction of gunpowder from China, helped concentrate power in a few hands.

Among the new nation-states was Portugal, which in 1384 won its independence from Castile under the leadership of John I. In 1435, at the close of the Hundred Years' War, Louis XI united France. With the 1469 marriage of Isabella of Castile and Ferdinand II of Aragon, Spain also became a unified state. And England came under the command of a single monarch, Henry VII, in 1485, after 30 years of the Wars of the Roses. Each of these states—especially Spain under the ambitious Isabella—sought to expand its sphere of influence through imperialism. Europe's taste for empire would soon be excited by the first voyage of Christopher Columbus.

ADMIRAL OF THE OCEAN SEA

Born in 1451, Christopher Columbus (Cristoforo Colombo) grew up in a middle-class family of woolen weavers in the Italian port city of Genoa and went to sea at an early age. A self-taught expert in geography, Columbus became convinced it was possible to reach the Indies by sailing west across the Atlantic Ocean. Around 1483 he developed his "Empresa de las Indias" (Enterprise of the Indies), a plan to discover a westward sea route to Asia.

In 1486 Columbus presented his plan to Spain's Queen Isabella, who turned it over to a commission of experts. The queen's Talavera Commission took four years to reject the Enterprise of the Indies as impractical. Columbus, however, did not give up. Finally, when the expulsion of the Moors from Granada revitalized Spain's religious fervor and national pride, Isabella decided to back Columbus's venture. She named him admiral of the ocean sea and viceroy and governor of any lands he discovered, and promised him a 10 percent share of all wealth that came from those lands.

After outfitting three ships and a crew of about 90 men, Columbus set sail from the port of Palos on August 3, 1492. The *Niña,* the *Pinta,*

Christopher Columbus presents his "Empresa de las Indias" to Queen Isabella's Talavera Commission. (Picture Collection, The Branch Libraries, The New York Public Library)

and the *Santa Maria* sailed west on unknown waters, out of sight of land for twice as long as most Europeans considered safe. Several weeks into the voyage, the frightened crew of the *Santa Maria* mutinied, but Columbus kept order by pledging to abort the expedition if it did not reach land within three days. Three days later, at about 2 A.M. on October 12, the lookout on the *Pinta* sighted land.

No one knows for sure where Columbus first made landfall in America, but most experts theorize it was on a small island in the central Bahamas, probably Watlings Island or Samana Cay. However, Columbus's previous calculations of the transatlantic distance from Europe to Asia told him he had attained his goal. In his log, he reported that he had reached Cipangu (Japan) and was off the coast of China: "It is certain that this is terra firma and that I am off Zayto and Qyinsay a hundred leagues more or less." He named the island San Salvador, although he noted the local people called it Guanahani.

The expedition next headed south along the Bahamas to Cuba, then east to Hispaniola. Along the way, Columbus wrote, he "found many islands filled with innumerable people, and I have taken possession of them all for their Highnesses, done by proclamation and with the royal standard unfurled, and no opposition was offered to me." The "innumerable people" Columbus met were Arawaks, whom he called *los Indios* in the mistaken belief he was in the Indies. He described them as gentle, peaceful, generous and intelligent as well as good-looking and healthy.

Columbus and his crew traded with the Arawaks whenever they spotted one wearing gold jewelry. Although he found none of the dazzling riches he expected to come across, Columbus was thrilled at the sight of gold, however limited. In his report to Isabella and Ferdinand, he exaggerated the wealth of the Arawaks so his trip would be deemed a success:

Your Highnesses should resolve to make them Christians, for I believe that if you begin, in a little while you will achieve the conversion of a great number of peoples to our holy faith, with the acquisition of great lordships and riches and all their inhabitants for Spain. For without a doubt there is a very great amount of gold in these lands. . . .

On Christmas Eve, the *Santa Maria* ran aground off the northern coast of Hispaniola. Columbus left 40 volunteers at a settlement named La Navidad and returned to Europe in the two remaining ships, taking seven captive Arawaks with him. The expedition reached Spain on March 15, 1493, 224 days after the start of the venture. News of Columbus's trip, especially of the presence of gold on the islands he reached, turned Europe's attention to the west.

The race was on. Almost immediately, Spain sent Columbus on a second voyage. He expanded Spain's claims in the Caribbean on that trip and on two later journeys. Portugal, meanwhile, launched its own expeditions; Pedro Álvares Cabral sighted the coast of Brazil in 1500. Before long, European explorers realized the lands Columbus had stumbled upon were not the Indies but an entirely different place previously unknown to them. They named the region America in honor of Florentine merchant Amerigo Vespucci, who sailed the coast from Mexico to Brazil for Spain in 1499. They also called it the New World.

CHAPTER TWO NOTES

p. 20   "An age will come . . ." Quoted in George Brown Tindall. *America: A Narrative History* (New York: W. W. Norton, 1988), 2nd ed., vol. 1, p. 10.

p. 21   "The voyage you wish . . ." Quoted in Eric Williams. *From Columbus to Castro: The History of the Caribbean* (New York: Vintage Books, 1984), p. 14.

pp. 27–28 "It is certain . . ." Quoted in Ted Morgan. *Wilderness at Dawn: The Settling of the North American Continent* (New York: Simon & Schuster, 1993), p. 49.

p. 28   ". . . found many islands . . ." Quoted in Winthrop D. Jordan, et al. *The United States: Conquering a Continent* (Englewood Cliffs, NJ: Prentice-Hall, 1987), 6th ed., vol. 1, p. 9.

p. 28   "Your Highnesses should . . ." Quoted in John M. Blum, et al. *The National Experience, Part I: A History of the United States to 1877* (San Diego: Harcourt Brace Jovanovich, 1989), 7th ed., p. 6.

CHAPTER 3

NEW SPAIN

News of Columbus's voyage started a veritable stampede of European explorers, missionaries, soldiers, and traders to America. Spain, the first nation to establish outposts in the Caribbean, dominated the first century of European enterprise in the New World. The Spanish came to consume the resources—especially the gold and silver—of the Americas and viewed the indigenous people they found there primarily as a source of labor to be turned into slaves or serfs. Missionaries hoped to convert Indian souls to Catholicism; soldiers often viewed them as vermin to be exterminated.

At first, the Indians greeted the newcomers with friendly generosity, but when the Spanish conquistadores turned out to be cruel and greedy, the Indians began to fight to defend their cultures. Equipped with firearms, armor, and horses, the invaders easily took what they wanted from American soil. They built little and produced nothing, and eventually the depletion of resources weakened the Spanish grip on its far-flung claims. Rather than easing the lot of the Indians, Spain's waning power in its more remote settlements allowed other European nations to force their way in and take a piece of the New World for themselves.

As it took over the Caribbean islands, Spain also sent numerous expeditions to the continent. Hernando Cortés conquered Mexico

AN ISLAND EMPIRE

Columbus brought sugarcane to the West Indies from the Canary Islands on his second voyage, in 1493, for enslaved Arawak Indians to cultivate. Hispaniola, where the first sugar mill was built in 1516, became the center of Caribbean sugar agriculture. Soon the industry spread to Jamaica, Puerto Rico, and Cuba. The Spanish also sought gold and silver on the islands, forcing Arawaks to perform the hard labor of mining.

By 1515 Hispaniola boasted 17 Spanish towns. As the Spanish prospered, the Indians died rapidly from disease, massacre, and overwork. Arriving as a missionary to Cuba with conquistador Diego Velázquez in 1511, a Dominican friar named Bartholomé de Las Casas was the first Catholic priest ordained in the New World. He found Spanish treatment of the Indians shockingly brutal and in 1515 petitioned King Ferdinand to offer them some protection. A few royal proclamations provided a measure of relief, but almost all the Caribbean Indians (perhaps as many as 6 million) were dead

from 1518 to 1522, arriving near present-day Veracruz with 555 soldiers and 16 horses. His European equipment allowed for a quick victory over the Aztecs, whose fabulous wealth Cortés plundered and sent back to Spain. Mexico City rose on the site of the destroyed Aztec capital, Tenochtitlán, and a period of conquistador domination began. Flocking to the region in search of more gold, conquistadores swept through the mountains and rain forests. In 1532 Francisco Pizarro entered Peru and toppled the gold-rich Inca Empire.

Spain formally established its Mexican colony in 1535, calling it the Viceroyalty of New Spain. Enslaved to dig for gold, many Indians of New Spain died from imported European diseases. But during the 1600s Mexican mines nonetheless produced staggering quantities of gold and silver that were sent back to Spain.

within a few years. In 1552 Las Casas wrote his *Brief Relation of the Destruction of the Indies,* in which he provided a vivid picture of the horrors wrought by the Spanish on the Arawaks and Caribs: "They [the Spanish] came with their Horsemen well armed with Sword and Launce, making most cruel Havocks [destruction] and slaughters . . . Overrunning Cities and Villages, where they spared no sex nor age. . . ."

As the sugar and mining industries grew and the supply of Indian slave labor shrank, the Spanish briefly attempted to use white slaves and convict labor in the Caribbean. When forced white labor failed to fill the gap, the Spanish began to import African captives. The Africans died as quickly as the Indians had, but slavers simply delivered more. Slave labor allowed the growth of large sugar plantations. Although the mines were depleted by the end of the 16th century, the sugar industry became hugely profitable. England and France started to eye the islands. They also sent ships to engage in piracy against Spanish galleons traversing the Caribbean with cargos of gold from Spain's exploits in Mexico and Central and South America.

The bounty of precious metals found in Mexico and Peru prompted rumors of other wealthy civilizations in the New World. These rumors evolved into the legend of El Dorado, a place said to be richer in gold than any country found before. Powerfully motivated by the prosect of gold, conquistadores steadily expanded the limits of New Spain's frontiers. Their wandering and plundering led them far afield, so that at its greatest extent in the 1770s, New Spain reached north through what is now Arizona and New Mexico to the San Francisco Bay area, east along the gulf to Texas and south to Guatemala. It also included a large portion of what is now the southeastern United States.

LA FLORIDA

Spain's first foray into territory now occupied by the United States occurred on the Florida peninsula in 1513. Drawn by tales of a

Fountain of Youth said to exist on an island north of Cuba, Juan Ponce de León, the former governor of Puerto Rico, received a commission from King Ferdinand to discover new lands. Sailing north, he first sighted the eastern Florida coast somewhere between present-day Cape Canaveral and Daytona Beach. His journey south down the Atlantic coast, around the keys, and north up the gulf coast convinced de León that he had found an island, which he promptly named La Florida. Along the way, his search for the Fountain of Youth was fruitless. This disappointment, and two Indian attacks, sent him back to Cuba.

After de León's departure, Spanish slave catchers frequented the Florida coast, abusing and kidnapping the Calusa Indians. The Calusas, in turn, looted Spanish ships grounded during storms and attacked any strangers who appeared. Efforts to establish Spanish settlements in Florida were thus ill-fated. When de León returned in 1521 to set up a colony, the Calusas resisted and killed him. The colony of 500 settlers founded by Lucas Vásquez de Ayllón in 1526 vanished without a trace.

A particularly cruel and inept conquistador led the next Spanish venture in Florida. Along with four ships, 400 people, and 80 horses, Pánfilo de Narváez arrived at Tampa Bay from Cuba in 1528. At first he came upon no Indians, for they had wisely gone into hiding. Narváez boldly went ashore to claim the land for Spain and sent his ships on to look for a good harbor. Then the Indians returned and, according to the conquistador, "made signs and menaces, and appeared to say we must go away from their country." Ignoring the Indian warning, Narváez advanced inland with 260 foot soldiers and 40 armed horsemen.

Skilled archers, the Apalachee Indians attacked his group repeatedly with bows so strong no Spaniard could bend them, reducing the contingent to 242. When the beleaguered Spanish made their way to Apalachee Bay to rendezvous with their ships, they found no one there to meet them. They were forced to make their own fragile boats and flee into the Gulf of Mexico. The doomed expedition unintentionally launched the first Spanish exploration of the American Southwest, which is described in the next section. (See p. 37.)

Despite Spanish failures to build a single settlement in Florida, Spain claimed it as part of its empire and named Hernando de Soto its governor in 1536. Subsequent attempts to establish missions and colonies in the region foundered because of fierce resistance by Indians familiar with Spanish brutality. As it turned out, the French were the first to gain a Florida beachhead. Jean Ribaut arrived there in 1562 to found a colony of French Huguenots. As he sailed up the coast, the French philosophy of cooperation with the Indians enabled him to establish friendly relations with the local people. Ribaut's Charlesfort settlement at the southern tip of South Carolina collapsed, but his efforts smoothed the path for the next French colonists in Florida.

In 1564 René de Laudonnière set up the settlement of Fort Caroline among friendly Indians at the mouth of the St. John's River. As French demands on the Indians for food and supplies grew heavier, the Indians turned hostile. Reinforcements arrived from France in 1565, but by then the Spanish got wind of French activity in Florida. Pedro Menendez de Avilés led a fleet of warships to the area and set up a base that would become St. Augustine, now the oldest permanent settlement in the United States. Menendez massacred the French settlers, reestablishing Spain's claims on Florida. Spanish settlement went no further, though. Efforts to set up military posts and Jesuit mission stations in Florida and as far north as Chesapeake Bay were frustrated by Indians defending their homeland.

The Spanish originally used the term *La Florida* to refer to all territory north of Mexico, but as exploration continued, only the southeastern portion of the present-day United States went by that name. Assisted by Luis de Moscoso de Alvaro, Governor Hernando de Soto sailed from Cuba to Tampa Bay in 1539 with seven ships carrying 570 men and 223 horses. De Soto intended to establish the Viceroyalty of Florida and to search for Cibola, a fabled land of great riches much talked about in New Spain. His ships had to fight their way up the peninsula, for hostile Apalachee Indians used signal fires to warn those ahead.

In the spring de Soto struck out through gulf country, terrorizing Indian villages as he went. He seized the people's food and pearls, forced the men to work as carriers and guides, and used the women as prostitutes. As captive chiefs led them from village to village, the Spaniards spread European diseases such as smallpox, bubonic plague, scarlet fever, typhus, cholera, measles, and diptheria among

Spanish conquistadores slaughter Native Americans. (Picture Collection, The Branch Libraries, The New York Public Library)

the Indians, who had no natural resistance to them. De Soto crashed through Creek, Cherokee, and Choctaw country, inciting an Indian attack at Mobile Bay. The Indians almost won, but de Soto burned their town and killed almost all its inhabitants. The encounter left many Spanish dead or wounded.

De Soto headed north into Chickasaw land, where cold and hunger killed more of his soldiers. Before he left in the spring of 1541, he tried to take women and slaves from the Indians. The ensuing battle killed most of the expedition's horses. But the Spanish crossed the Mississippi River into what is now Arkansas, plundering Indian towns almost to the Oklahoma border. Near the junction of the Red River and the Mississippi, de Soto contracted a fever and died in the spring of 1542. The expedition continued its ravages in Louisiana, east Texas, and Arkansas until it sailed down the Mississippi to the gulf in the summer of 1543. Only 311 survivors made it back to Mexico.

During the 1600s the Spanish managed to gain control over the Indians of present-day Florida and southern Georgia. By 1634 the area was home to 30 Spanish missionaries, 44 missionary stations, and 30,000 Indian converts to Catholicism. The Spanish put down a minor revolt in 1656, and their hold on Florida would not be challenged again until the arrival of other Europeans.

THE SOUTHWEST

The first Europeans to venture into the terrain now occupied by the southwestern United States came there by accident. Fleeing the hostile Apalachees of Florida, the 242 survivors of the Narváez expedition (see page 34) were shipwrecked in the fall of 1528 near present-day Galveston, Texas. Most of the men, including Narváez, drowned, but about 80 were cast ashore. Although helped by friendly local Indians, all but four of the Spaniards eventually died.

Among the survivors were Álvar Núñez Cabeza de Vaca and a Moorish slave named Estevanico. Taken in by the Indians, the men served as near slaves for six years. They finally escaped and headed west. When they reached the Rio Grande near present-day El Paso, they heard tales of Cibola, the same golden land sought by de Soto in the Southeast. They continued west across New Mexico and Arizona, then turned south down a trading trail through Mexico's Sonora Valley. By the time they reached Spanish territory, in 1536, Cabeza de Vaca had gained deep respect for Native American culture and was distressed by the abuse the Spanish so casually dispensed to the Mexicans. He soon returned to Spain.

His fellow wanderers, however, stayed in New Spain and thrilled Mexico City with embellished tales of wealth to the north. A preliminary expedition formed to investigate the claims. Led by a Franciscan monk, Fray Marcos de Niza, and guided by Estevanico, it left Mexico City in 1539. Dispatched as a scout, Estevanico sent back reports of finding the seven great cities of Cibola. In fact, he came upon Hawikuh, the westernmost Zuñi pueblo. Estevanico's arrogant assertion of authority angered the Indians there, who told him to leave. Instead he advanced on the pueblo and was killed. The rest of his group rejoined Marcos and the expedition returned to Mexico City. Prone to exaggeration, Marcos told of the north's large, wealthy cities, feeding Spanish hopes of finding El Dorado.

In 1540, at the age of 30, Francisco Vásquez de Coronado started north accompanied by an army of well-equipped horsemen and foot soldiers in their teens and twenties. His orders from the Mexican viceroy were to claim new land for the crown without hurting or robbing the Indians they found there. In this effort he was assisted by García López de Cárdenas and advised by Fray Marcos, whom he soon found out was a liar. "We have all become very distrustful of the father provincial," he wrote, "and were dismayed to see that everything was the reverse of what he said."

Aware that the Spanish were approaching, the Pueblo Indians prepared to defend themselves. They rejected Coronado's peaceful overtures and attacked his camp at midnight, but the Spanish repelled them and advanced. Near Hawikuh, several hundred Zuñi warriors blocked Coronado's way. The conquistadores attacked and, equipped with superior arms, captured the pueblo in an hour, although Coronado was badly wounded. The Spanish occupied the pueblo for six months and eventually made peace with the local Indians.

From his base at Hawikuh, Coronado sent contingents to subdue the Hopi pueblos and to look for a "great river" of which the Indians spoke. On that mission Cárdenas found the Colorado River and the Grand Canyon. Other Indians told of buffalo plains to the east; Pedro de Alvarado set out with them to investigate. Alvarado's party came across the great Acoma pueblo, the Rio Grande, and numerous pueblos in an area he called Tiguex, which lay between present-day Albuquerque and Taos.

About this time Coronado heard of Quivira, a gold-rich land to the northeast. He decided to move his headquarters to Tiguex, where he evicted Indians from their pueblos. The Spanish took what they wanted from the Pueblo people and harassed them for information about Quivira. When the Indians rebelled, Coronado and Cárdenas destroyed the pueblos, burned captives at the stake, and enslaved those whom they did not kill.

Intentionally misled by his Indian guides, Coronado wandered the high plains of the Texas panhandle in search of Quivira and met friendly but poor Apache. The conquistador eventually confronted his guides and learned the truth about his destination. He headed northeast to central Kansas, where he found Quivira. Much to his disappointment, it was not a gold-paved country but a cluster of Wichita hunting and farming villages consisting of grass-covered lodges. Coronado killed his one remaining guide in disgust and returned to Mexico in 1542. Standing trial there for cruelty to Indians, Coronado was acquitted but Cárdenas was found guilty.

The Spanish now realized Pueblo country was no El Dorado and did not try to conquer it again for 40 years. During that time, various conquistadores haphazardly destroyed villages, killed Indians, and captured slaves there, but they made no effort at colonization. Not until 1595 did Spain develop a serious plan for settling the region.

Juan de Oñate was placed in charge of the effort, with Vincente de Zaldivar as his second-in-command. In 1598 they led a group of 400 settlers north from Mexico. The Pueblo Indians fled before the advancing Spanish, who found empty country of no value to them. At a place called Santo Domingo, north of present-day Albuquerque, Oñate finally met with representatives from 31 pueblos and proclaimed them and the people they represented Spanish subjects. He then established his headquarters, called San Gabriel, at the San Juan pueblo north of Española on the Chama River. Dividing the land between the Great Plains and the Hopi pueblos into districts, Oñate assigned friars to each and set up estates for the Spanish settlers.

Oñate and Zaldivar destroyed a number of pueblos, killed hundreds of people, and took hundreds more captive. More and more Indians fled to the mountains, where many starved or froze to death. The depopulation left the colonists with no means of support, and many returned to Mexico in 1601. In the disorder many Indian captives escaped. By 1604 a fragile truce was reached, but the failure of the colony forced Oñate back to Mexico. Pedro de Peralta was appointed governor in 1609. Founding Santa Fe as its capital in 1610, he imported 250 Spanish colonists and 700 Mexican slaves and set about building a permanent colony.

Ongoing Spanish abuse fueled mounting Indian hostility as the 1600s progressed. Many Indians secretly continued to practice the traditional customs, beliefs, and ceremonies that had been outlawed by the Spanish. One such Indian, a medicine man named Popé, spearheaded the Great Pueblo Revolt of 1680. Popé held secret meetings with representatives from other pueblos and sent messengers out to spread news of his plan. On the designated date, Pueblo Indians throughout the colony burned churches and killed more than 400 Spanish friars, soldiers, and colonists. They then joined with the Apache to surround Santa Fe and demanded freedom for all Indian slaves. The Spanish were forced to retreat to the Rio Grande, and

Pueblo country remained free for 13 years. One disgusted friar who visited the Southwest during this period wrote of the Indians, "They have been found to be so pleased with liberty of conscience and so attached to the worship of Satan that up to the present not a sign has been visible of their ever having been Christians."

Unfortunately, Popé became a tyrant; in addition, without Spanish protection the pueblos were vulnerable to Apache raids. The Apaches had obtained horses from the Spanish, and soon the Ute, Shoshoni, and Plateau and Plains tribes acquired them as well. Raiding and plague weakened the Pueblo towns, so by the time Francisco de Vargas was appointed governor in 1692, they were easily overpowered. Only a few Pueblo Indians managed to escape to Navajo or Apache territory. The Hopi were never reconquered, but the rest of the Pueblo rebellion was crushed by 1698.

Under Spanish colonialism, the governor appointed alcaldes (mayors) to oversee each pueblo. The colonists imported domestic animals, fruit trees, and farm implements, changing the Indian way of life forever. The pueblos paid tribute to their alcaldes in the form of beans, maize, butter, and sheep; Indians also were forced to farm, weave, and keep house for the Spanish. Catholic padres, meanwhile, did what they could to stamp out traditional beliefs. To further weaken both the Pueblo peoples and the Apache, the Spanish cultivated warfare between them. Because fighting disrupted trade between the settled groups and the nomadic Apache, the Apache were forced to rely on raiding for survival. The Navajo also engaged in some raiding.

Spanish settlement eventually extended east into present-day Texas and almost as far as the Mississippi River. But throughout the Southwest, Spanish colonial growth was slow. The colonial outposts remained relatively isolated until the influx of other white settlers in the 19th century.

CALIFORNIA

Hernando Cortés, the first Spaniard to sight the Baja coast, gave California its name in 1535. But not until Juan Rodríguez Cabrillo and Bartolomé Ferrelo sailed north from Mexico's west coast in 1542 did Europeans reach the land that now makes up the State of California.

Sir Francis Drake. (Library of Congress)

A number of other explorers further strengthened the Spanish claim to California.

The English, however, did not recognize that claim. Commissioned by Queen Elizabeth I in 1577, Sir Francis Drake sailed out as a privateer in the New World to pillage Spain's wealth. Sacking Spanish ships and settlements for gold, he made his way down the east coast and up the west coast of South and Central America. Drake then sailed north to the coast of what is now Oregon, reaching it in June 1579. As he sailed south down the coast of California, he came upon a harbor just north of present-day San Francisco, which he named Drake's Bay. The peaceful, friendly local Indians treated the English sailors royally. Claiming the land for England, Drake wrote that he "set up a monument of our being there . . . a plate of brasse, fast nailed to a great and firm post." He reached England with the news on September 26, 1580.

By then England had made significant inroads into Spanish claims in America. Seeking an ever bigger piece of the New World, Queen Elizabeth sent Drake back across the Atlantic to engage in more piracy against Spanish ships. On this expedition Drake became a leader in the fighting between English and Spanish ships in the Caribbean. England finally destroyed the Spanish Armada (naval fleet) in 1588 and evicted Spain from most of the Caribbean. From then on, Spain would play only a minor role in the conquest of North America.

CHAPTER THREE NOTES

p. 33   "They [the Spanish] came . . ." Quoted in Alvin M. Josephy, Jr. *The Indian Heritage of America* (Boston: Houghton Mifflin, 1968), p. 287.

p. 34   ". . . made signs and menaces . . ." Quoted in Angie Debo. *A History of the Indians of the United States* (Norman, OK: University of Oklahoma Press, 1970), p. 21.

p. 38   "We have all become . . ." Quoted in Morgan. p. 76.

p. 40   "They have been found . . ." Quoted in Debo. p. 50.

p. 42   ". . . set up a monument . . ." Quoted in Samuel Eliot Morison. *The European Discovery of America: The Southern Voyages* (New York: Oxford University Press, 1974), p. 667.

FRANCE IN THE
NEW WORLD

Although it never established a large North American population, France played a vital role in the conquest of North America. In the process of building the highly profitable fur trade, French immigrants to the New World opened an enormous amount of territory to European incursion. Traveling between far-flung French trading posts and forts from Newfoundland to New Orleans, a small, mobile population of trappers, traders, missionaries, and explorers mingled with rather than displaced the indigenous people they encountered. Through the 17th century, the large majority of French immigrants were men who came without families to partake of the continent's wildness, not to tame it. Among them were the fiercely independent *coureurs de bois* (runners of the woods), or *voyageurs* (travelers), who lived in the forests, adopted Indian survival techniques, and pursued their fortunes in the fur trade.

The earliest French settlements, such as Jean Ribaut's 1562 attempt to found a colony of Huguenot dissidents at Charlesfort in present-day South Carolina and René de Laudonnière's 1564 settlement of Fort Caroline in Florida (see Chapter 3), failed miserably. During the 16th century, France concentrated instead on finding a route around North America to the Indies (the so-called Northwest Passage) and on exploiting America's natural wealth. But by 1600, aware of England's preoccupation with the new continent, King Henry IV determined that France should colonize America before its rival did. He offered financial enticements to investors willing to back such a venture, but few French subjects had any desire to leave their homeland. Those who did were interested more in turning a profit than in turning the wilderness into a home.

French settlements eventually took root in the region the French called Acadia (present-day Nova Scotia, New Brunswick, and western Newfoundland) and along the St. Lawrence River in present-day Quebec. Together with the Great Lakes region, these two territories made up New France. Along the Gulf of Mexico near the mouth of the Mississippi River, the French established settlements at Mobile (Alabama), Biloxi (Mississippi), and New Orleans. The first Europeans to travel the length of the Mississippi, they claimed all the lands drained by the great river. Stretching from the Great Lakes to the Gulf of Mexico and from the Appalachian Mountains to the Rocky Mountains, this vast expanse was called Louisiana.

Between the settlements of New France and those of coastal Louisiana, the French established only a few forts and trading posts. Because the French did not attempt to establish alien rule over the Indians, and because the settlers were too few in number to push the Indians off their land or kill off their game, they managed to remain friendly with most Indians. This helped France secure control of the waterways that gave access to North America's interior. With a firm grip on the St. Lawrence River, French traders could sail from the Atlantic Ocean to the Gulf of Mexico via the Great Lakes and the Mississippi River—and could prevent anyone else from doing the same. Motion, not rest, was to be the French legacy in the New World.

THE SIXTEENTH CENTURY

The first French venture in North America was an attempt to find the Northwest Passage to Cathay (China). Backed by a group of Italian expatriates and King Francis I, Florentine navigator Giovanni da Verrazano sailed west from France in 1523. In 1524 Verrazano made his first landfall, at present-day Cape Fear, North Carolina. He then sailed up the coast, making a brief stop at present-day New York Harbor before moving on to Newfoundland. Verrazano scouted the coast but did not explore it, and returned to France convinced North America was a new continent.

Rumors about the riches to be found on the new continent circulated throughout Europe. In 1532 Francis I sponsored another voyage to investigate these rumors, sending Jacques Cartier to discover a new land "where it is said that a great quantity of gold, and other precious things, are to be found." Cartier sailed to Newfoundland and the Gulf of St. Lawrence in 1534, reaching the Gaspé Peninsula of present-day Quebec. At Gaspé Bay Cartier captured Donnacona, the chief of the Iroquois band who met the French, got him drunk, and convinced him they meant no harm. Two of Donnacona's sons returned to France with Cartier, where the king was so pleased that he sent the explorer on another trip.

In 1535 Cartier returned to North America with the chief's sons. The Indians guided him to the St. Lawrence River, which he conjectured might be the Northwest Passage. He reached the Indian village of Stadacona at the site where Quebec City now stands and sailed on to the Indian village of Hochelaga, at the site of present-day Montreal. There the Indians greeted him so warmly that Cartier extolled them on paper. "One of the most attractive features of Indian society," he wrote, "was the spirit of hospitality by which it was pervaded. Perhaps no people ever carried this principle to the same degree as the Iroquois."

At Hochelaga, Cartier climbed a peak he named Mount Royal in order to survey the river ahead. Seeing that dangerous rapids lay before him, he returned to Stadacona for the winter. In the extreme cold, lacking a proper diet, 25 Frenchmen died before the Indians showed them how to make a medicine rich in vitamin C. Donnacona regaled Cartier with stories about a nearby land called Saguenay, where a race of white people possessed untold wealth in gold, silver, rubies, and spices. Eager to look for Saguenay, the explorer returned to France in 1536 for more financing. With him were ten kidnapped Indians, including Donnacona, who thrilled Cartier's backers with his descriptions of Saguenay. All ten Indians soon died of the common cold, to which they had no immunity.

Francis I appointed a nobleman, the sieur de Roberval, viceroy of Saguenay and gave his blessing to Cartier's third expedition. Roberval and Cartier arrived in Quebec in 1541 with 200 settlers—mostly convicts—aboard five ships. The Indians were alarmed by the whites' obvious intention to settle in their territory. They launched sporadic attacks on the settlers throughout the winter while the settlers coped with hunger and illness. By spring 35 Frenchmen were dead. A disgusted Cartier abandoned the settlement and returned to France. Roberval took command, but a year later he had still seen no evidence of the existence of Saguenay. In 1543 he gave up and went home. It was almost 60 years before the French officially returned to North America.

During that time, however, fishing expeditions from all parts of Europe tapped the burgeoning fishing banks of Newfoundland. Independent trappers and traders, many of them from France, made their way into the interior and sent a steady stream of beaver, otter, and other pelts back to Europe. Using beaver pelts imported from North America, hat makers in Paris and Amsterdam started making fine felt hats that became a European fashion phenomenon at the turn of the 17th century. Demand for American furs skyrocketed.

THE COMPANY OF NEW FRANCE

Hoping to lock in French control of the fur trade, Pierre du Gua, sieur de Monts, and a group of other wealthy Frenchmen organized the Company of New France. Under its agreement with the king, the company would keep 90 percent of its profit and give 10 percent to the crown. In 1604 the company recruited Samuel de Champlain to spearhead its efforts in New France.

Champlain sailed to North America with 79 emigrés under the command of de Monts. The group settled on Île St. Croix, which now lies in Maine on the New Brunswick border. After a bad winter killed 34 of the settlers, Champlain set out in search of a more hospitable site for a settlement and trading post. He explored the coast from New Brunswick to Massachusetts in 1605 and recommended a move to Port Royal (present-day Annapolis Royal) on Nova Scotia. Marc Lescarbot, a settler at Port Royal, described the trading post as a place where the men enjoyed themselves and commerce with the Indians was brisk.

"When winter came," he wrote, "the savages of the country assembled at Port Royal from far and near to barter . . . some bringing beaver and other skins . . . also moose skins, of which excellent buff jackets may be made, others bringing fresh meat." The settlement held its own, but in 1607 the company decided to abandon it because they could not compete with Basques and other independent traders who trafficked in furs illegally.

The French, however, did not give up on Acadia. In 1610 Jean de Biencourt de Poutrincourt and Claude de Saint Étienne de la Tour rebuilt Port Royal. With Poutrincourt as governor, French settlers established a permanent foothold. By then the region's indigenous people were dying out. European disease was one culprit; French manipulation of tribal rivalries was another. To strengthen their own hold on the land, whites encouraged the Indians to fight with each other, hoping they would kill each other off. The strategy was chillingly effective against the Beothuk of Newfoundland. After a Frenchman shot a Beothuk in 1613, the Beothuk killed 37 fishermen in the area. The French armed the Micmac, longtime enemies of the Beothuk, and offered bounties for Beothuk scalps. The practice almost completely obliterated the Beothuk people.

The French also faced conflict with other Europeans. In 1613 two Jesuit missionaries arrived on Saint Saveur Island, near Mt. Desert Island in Maine. England had already claimed Maine and viewed the move as an invasion. Captain Samuel Argall evicted the French from Saint Saveur and sailed north to sack Port Royal. Standing firm, Poutrincourt and his son, Charles de Biencourt, rebuilt Port Royal, and in 1624 Charles de Saint Étienne de la Tour (Claude's son) was named governor. The new governor immediately took measures to defend against the English, building a fort at Cap du Sable on Nova Scotia's southern tip.

While Acadia's fortunes rose and fell, Quebec emerged along the St. Lawrence. The Huron Indians became the main partners of the French in the fur trade. In 1608 Champlain founded Quebec City with 25 settlers, all but nine of whom died during their difficult first winter at the site. The following year the explorer ventured up the St. Lawrence almost as far as Hochelaga, then headed south and came upon the lake to which he gave his name. There he joined a Huron war party

A drawing by Champlain of the 1609 Indian battle in which the explorer and his party participated. (National Archives of Canada)

in an attack against the Onondaga tribe of the Iroquois League, which had sought to divert furs away from the Huron into their own hands. Equipped with European firearms, Champlain helped the Huron defeat the Iroquois easily. He later described the attack: "When I saw them making a move to fire at us, I rested my musket against my cheek and aimed directly at one of the three chiefs. With the same shot two fell to the ground; and one of their men was so wounded that he died some time after." Champlain's action sparked a lasting Iroquois animosity toward the French. On a 1615 expedition to the Great Lakes, Champlain was wounded in a fight with some Iroquois and was forced to return to France.

In 1627 Quebec had only 55 French settlers. Champlain tried to interest French investors in financing the permanent settlement of Quebec, but they were attracted to New France by fur-trade profits rather than colonial progress. Champlain finally found backing from the Company of 100 Associates, with the proviso that only French Catholics would be permitted to colonize New France. But most French Catholics were happy in their homeland: It was religious dissidents such as the Huguenots (and many people from other countries) who hungered to build a life elsewhere. The company's policy thereby crippled the development of New France.

Champlain was further hobbled by the outbreak of war between France and England in 1627. In 1628 he sailed to North America with four ships and 400 colonists, but the English captured them and then took Quebec City in 1629. England acquired New France, although French resistance persisted in Acadia. New France was returned to France in 1632 under the treaty of Saint-Germain-en-Laye.

Champlain returned to Quebec to pursue his development plan. Settlement there remained sparse, with most immigrants arriving involuntarily from French prisons and poorhouses. French explorers continued to expand white knowledge of the continent, and the settlement of Trois-Rivières was founded in 1634, but at Champlain's death in 1635, there were still only 150 colonists along the St. Lawrence. Nevertheless, Indians threatened by smallpox epidemics and the disruptions of the fur trade sensed that white settlers would soon overcome them. According to records left by Champlain, one chief told him:

I am but a tiny animal that crawls on the earth. You French are the great of this world. . . . You will build a house that is a fortress, then you will build another house . . . and then we will be nothing but dogs that sleep outdoors. . . . You will grow wheat, and we will no longer look for our sustenance in the woods, we will be no better than vagabonds.

In all New France, there were 300 white traders, fishermen, and missionaries by 1640. These few adventurers cast their net wide, building posts and missions among the Ottawa, Ojibwa, Fox, and other Indian tribes with whom they formed alliances. Despite the peaceful relations between the French and the Indians, the white arrival did serious harm to Indian culture. Intense rivalry among tribes for fur-trade profits caused Indians to abandon their traditional respect for the game they hunted. Time-honored rituals of conservation died as overhunting became the rule. The white introduction of alcohol took a heavy toll on people who had never tasted it before. Drunkenness was frequent and often violent.

Catholic missionaries also had an impact on Indian culture. Some lived with the Indians and learned to respect their ways, while others sought only to wipe out beliefs and traditions they did not understand. Two of the more famous French missionaries to North America were Mère Marie de l'Incarnation (Marie Guyart), who in 1639 opened an Ursuline Convent in Quebec, and Paul de Chomedy, sieur de Maisonneuve, who founded Montreal in 1642. Another was Claude-Jean Allouez, a Jesuit missionary who traveled among 22 Indian tribes around the Great Lakes in 1669 and 1670. Allouez claimed to baptize 10,000 Indians during his trip. Well intentioned or not, the missionaries invariably spread disease among the Indians. Often blaming the missionaries for the new illnesses that brought death to their people, Indians sometimes killed them.

Epidemics of European disease drastically reduced the Huron population during the 1630s. This left them vulnerable to attack by the rival Iroquois, who took advantage of the situation to build their fur trade with the English. Throughout the 1640s, the Iroquois repeatedly pummeled the Huron. In 1648 and 1649 they launched a massacre of the Huron nation around Georgian Bay, then went on to crush the Tionontati to the west and the Neutral Confederacy of Lake Erie. Wherever and whenever they could, the Iroquois terrorized Indian allies of the French.

The Ottawa replaced the Huron as France's main ally in the fur trade, which expanded steadily to the Great Lakes and the upper Mississippi River. The fur trade eventually reached across the northern plains to the Rocky Mountains. In exchange for furs, the Indians of the lake and prairie country obtained guns. Those guns would prove pivotal in the conflicts that erupted as the frontiers of France, England, and Spain, collided in North America.

In one collision of frontiers, England took Acadia from France for the second time, in 1654. Acadia was once again restored to France in 1667; in the meantime, the Company of New France was disbanded and New France became a royal province in 1663. France sent Jean-Baptiste Colbert and Jean-Baptiste Talon to the colony in 1665 with orders to promote permanent settlement and economic development. They organized a government and worked to reduce the colony's dependence on the fur trade by stimulating economic diversification.

"NO LIFE SO HAPPY"

In 1825 a Canadian historian by the name of Alexander Ross traveled to the shores of Lake Winnipeg to interview a 70-year-old man who had spent his youth as a *coureur de bois*. The man recalled a life without worries, lived to the rhythm of songs sung while paddling canoes. Ross included the *voyageur's* reminiscences in his 1855 book, *The Fur Hunters of the Far West:*

> I have now been forty-two years in this country. For twenty-four I was a light canoe man. . . . No portage was too long for me; all portages were alike. My end of the canoe never touched the ground till I saw the end of [the portage] . . . . Fifty songs a day were nothing to me, I could carry, paddle, walk and sing with any man I ever saw. . . . No water, no weather, ever stopped the paddle or the song. I have had twelve wives in the country; and was once possessed of fifty horses, and six running dogs, trimmed in the first style. I was then like a Bourgeois, rich and happy: no Bourgeois had better dressed wives than I; no Indian chief finer horses; no white man better harnessed or swifter dogs. . . . I wanted for nothing; and I spent all my earnings in the enjoyment of pleasure. Five hundred pounds, twice told, have passed through my hands; although I now have not a spare shirt to my back, nor a penny to buy one. Yet, were I young again, I should glory in commencing the same career again. I would spend another half-century in the same fields of enjoyment. There is no life so happy as a voyageur's life; none so independent; no place where a man enjoys so much variety and freedom as in the Indian country.

As incentive for wandering trappers and fur traders to settle down and build communities, Colbert and Talon arranged for French women to be sent to New France to serve as wives. They also encouraged Frenchmen to marry Indian women. A brewery and a tannery were built, livestock and horses were imported, land was cleared, and France's seigneurial system of agriculture was introduced. Under this system, the government granted property to landlords called seigneurs, who found tenants to raise crops.

By 1666 New France north of the St. Lawrence had a population of nearly 6,000, but the Iroquois remained a threat to the colony. King Louis XIV sent four companies of the Carignan-Salières regiment, a total of 1,300 men, to resolve the situation. The move resulted in a fragile peace treaty in 1667. From that point on, France maintained a military presence in North America to protect its interests from the Iroquois and from the English.

LOUISIANA

In 1672 Louis de Buade, comte de Frontenac et Palluau, became governor of New France. Under his leadership, explorers reached Niagara Falls and St. Anthony's Falls, charted the Great Lakes, and traversed present-day Ontario. To combat growing British interference in the fur trade, the French built forts along strategic water routes throughout New France. Conflict with the Iroquois continued, and efforts to crush the Indians in the 1680s and 1690s failed. But New France grew: By 1690 the colony had a population of 15,000.

Frontenac's tenure as governor of New France was notable for his role in the exploration of the Mississippi River and the claiming of Louisiana. In 1672 Frontenac sent Louis Jolliet to explore the Great Lakes. Reaching the mission of Father Jacques Marquette, located between Lakes Michigan and Huron, Jolliet convinced the Jesuit to join him. Together they explored the Great Lakes and the Illinois River, then followed the Wisconsin River to the Mississippi. They traveled down the Mississippi as far as its juncture with the Arkansas River before turning back to avoid contact with Spaniards to the south. In honor of Louis XIV, they named the region they explored Louisiana.

René-Robert Cavelier de La Salle was the next Mississippi River explorer sponsored by Frontenac. An arrogant, unbalanced man who made a living selling liquor to the Indians, La Salle was disliked by almost all his fellow settlers. But in 1677, with the governor's support, he was authorized by Louis XIV to explore the interior of North America. In 1679 La Salle made a preliminary trip across the Great Lakes to the Illinois River. Three years later he made his way back to the Illinois and followed it to the Mississippi. Taking the river all the

Louis Jolliet and Father Jacques Marquette canoe along the Mississippi River in 1673.
(Picture Collection, The Branch Libraries, The New York Public Library)

way south, he reached the Gulf of Mexico. On behalf of France he laid claim to the entire area drained by the Mississippi and applied the name Louisiana. La Salle returned to Quebec and sailed for France with the good news.

In 1684 the king sent La Salle back to the New World to build forts along the Mississippi. La Salle sailed with four ships and 300 men, who grew increasingly distrustful of him because of his mental instability. Paranoid about unseen enemies and delusional about his own power, La Salle directed his ships across the Gulf of Mexico to find the mouth of the Mississippi. Sailing too far west, the fleet landed at Matagora Bay in Texas. Despite all the evidence to the contrary, La Salle was convinced he was in the Mississippi River delta.

La Salle lands at Matagora Bay in 1685 and mistakes it for part of the Mississippi River delta. (Library of Congress)

He built a fort, but disease and Indian attacks started to kill off his men. Twenty of them deserted and returned to France, but La Salle would not give up. He decided he had not sailed far enough west and struck out across Texas to find the Mississippi. More deranged with each passing week, he searched for the river until 1687, when one of his men finally killed him.

Jean-Baptiste Le Moyne, sieur de Bienville, was appointed governor of Louisiana, a post he filled on and off for almost 50 years, until 1743.

He oversaw the exploration of Louisiana by a number of French explorers, who charted the vast region's rivers. Ignoring the arid Southwest, Bienville concentrated on developing trade along the Mississippi and Missouri rivers, establishing a valuable alliance with the Choctaw Indians in the South. A few small farms and settlements appeared along the Mississippi, but most French activity in the interior centered around scattered trading posts.

The only major settlements established by the French in Louisiana were along the Gulf of Mexico. The governor's older brother, Pierre Le Moyne, sieur d'Iberville, set up a colony at Biloxi (Mississippi) and then established Mobile (Alabama) in 1710. In 1718 Bienville founded New Orleans at the mouth of the Mississippi. Hostilities with the Natchez Indians broke out in 1729. After the Natchez attacked Fort Rosalie, killing 200 Frenchmen, the French called on their Choctaw allies and killed almost all the Natchez. They sent 427 captives to Haiti as slaves.

Bienville's scorn for all Indians was equally apparent in his attempts to counter Chickasaw attacks on French boats traveling the Mississippi. The Indians frequently attacked boats passing Chickasaw Bluff near present-day Memphis. When diplomatic negotiations failed to end the attacks, the governor turned to the Choctaw for help. Bienville recorded the results in 1719:

> The Choctaws, whom I had set in motion against the Chickasaws, have destroyed entirely three villages of this ferocious Nation, which disturbed our commerce on the river. They have raised about four hundred scalps, and made one hundred prisoners. . . . a most important advantage which we have obtained, the more so, that it has not cost one drop of French blood, through the care I took of opposing those barbarians to one another. Their self-destruction operated in this manner is the sole efficacious way of insuring tranquility in the colony.

Louisiana became a royal province of France in 1732. In subsequent years Bienville continued his campaign against the Chickasaw, who by then had obtained guns from the English. His alliance with the Choctaw eroded during the 1730s, when some switched their allegiance to the English. A civil war broke out among the Choctaw in 1740, and the French stepped in to help those still loyal to them. After the pro-English Choctaw were defeated in 1750, all the Choctaw were subjected to direct French rule. The Chickasaw, however, eluded French domination and maintained their independence.

In 1750, the year of the Choctaw defeat, the French population of North America reached 80,000. These settlers were thinly spread over an enormous expanse of territory. For the most part, the French colonists failed to settle down and build stable communities. Inveterate traders, they continued to roam the continent without populating it. The French crown was frustrated with the still-temporary character of its colonies. And with good reason, it worried about the advancing tide of thriving, purposeful English colonists.

CHAPTER FOUR NOTES

p. 45   ". . . where it is said . . ." Quoted in J. M. Bumsted. *The Peoples of Canada: A Pre-Confederation History* (Toronto: Oxford University Press, 1992), p. 33.

p. 45   "One of the most . . ." Quoted in Morgan. p. 68.

p. 47   "When winter came . . ." Quoted in Debo. p. 38.

p. 48   "When I saw . . ." Quoted in Bumsted. p. 66.

p. 49   "I am but a tiny . . ." Quoted in Morgan. p. 104.

p. 51   "I have now been . . ." Quoted in William J. Eccles. *The Canadian Frontier, 1534–1760* (New York: Holt, Rhinehart and Winston, 1969), p. 191.

p. 55   "The Choctaws . . ." Quoted in Debo. p. 74.

THE ENGLISH COLONIES

Sir Francis Drake's voyage to California in 1579 (see Chapter 3) was an anomaly in Great Britain's conquest of North America. Other than that venture, by which Drake claimed the continent's West Coast in the name of Queen Elizabeth I, England approached America from the east. For almost a century after Columbus made his first voyage, the English concentrated on finding a northern route around the New World to the Indies—the so-called Northwest Passage. In the process, they learned much about the coastal geography and inhabitants of present-day Maritime Canada and New England. What they found eventually convinced them there was ample opportunity on the new continent to obtain wealth and glory for themselves, their country, and their God, even if they never found the Northwest Passage.

Exploration by France and Spain, nations that had gotten an earlier start in North America, convinced England of the necessity of securing its interests by establishing permanent settlements there. Some English speculators hoped to find rich North American kingdoms like those the Spanish had conquered in Mexico and Peru. Others wanted to develop the fur trade, to protect England's rights to the continent's Atlantic fishing banks and other natural resources, and to expand the market for English goods. Promoting Sir Walter Raleigh's plan to found England's first American colony, Richard Hakluyt told Queen Elizabeth that "our chiefe desire is to find out ample vent of our wollen cloth (the naturall commoditie of this our realme)."

In years to come, the crown would give its blessing to many colonizing ventures, but it left the planning and financing to private investors, who received patents from the crown to develop designated regions. The first such companies to be chartered came out of efforts by Sir Ferdinando Gorges. In 1606 King James I granted the North Virginia Company of Plymouth (headed by Gorges) the right to develop the northern part of the continent and the South Virginia Company of London the right to develop the southern part.

Eager to acquire European goods, Indians greeted the earliest English arrivals warmly. But in a pattern that would be repeated countless times as whites pushed across the continent, misunderstandings and mistreatment soon strained Indian-white relations. For the English, these tensions were more pronounced and prolonged than for their French and Spanish counterparts, because the English wanted to settle on Indian land rather than just travel across it. England's population pressures and unemployment problems sent families and farmers, rather than adventurers and traders, to its colonies.

Concentrated and growing rapidly, the English population in North America was a serious threat to the Indians. From a total of 2,000 in 1625, the population of the English colonies grew to 250,000 by 1700. The colonists followed a policy of divide and conquer, by which they promoted discord between Indians to weaken their defenses against the white invasion.

FIRST FORAYS

England's King Henry VII chartered John Cabot to find a westward route to Asia in 1497. A Venetian citizen (born Giovanni Caboto), Cabot was a merchant sailor who had moved to England in search of opportunity. Sailing to Newfoundland, which he believed to be a part of Asia, he became the first European to set foot on North American soil since the Vikings had abandoned their fishing village centuries ago.

Cabot claimed the land for England and explored its coast. Although he encountered no Indians, he saw that the sea swarmed with codfish. On his second voyage, in 1498, Cabot left England with five ships. One put in at Ireland in distress; the others were never heard from again.

During the 1500s fishermen from all over Europe sailed to the Grand Banks off Newfoundland, to the Gulf of St. Lawrence, and to the St. Lawrence River. A thriving seasonal fishing industry developed in the area, but no permanent settlements. English interest in the region remained focused on finding the Northwest Passage, and in 1576 the Muscovy Company (organized to trade with Russia) sent master mariner Martin Frobisher to seek a water route through the Canadian Arctic. Reaching Baffin Island, he found a bay (Frobisher Bay) that he thought was a strait and concluded that it must lead to the western sea.

Even more interesting to Frobisher's backers was a rock he brought back from the island. An authority of dubious expertise pronounced the rock gold-bearing, inspiring the investors to send Frobisher back to Baffin Island to look for more "gold ore." Sailing in 1577 with three ships and 120 men, he gathered 200 tons of rock. He kidnapped three Inuit and returned to England, where his rocks once again excited his backers. On one final journey to Baffin Island, in 1578, Frobisher collected yet more "ore." When he returned to England, however, all the rocks he had accumulated were discovered to be worthless and his American career came to an end.

In 1583 Sir Humphrey Gilbert made the first English effort to colonize Newfoundland. He took possession of the island for Queen Elizabeth, but as he was lost with his ship on the way back to England, nothing came of the venture. English luck was no better to the south. In 1584 Sir Walter Raleigh sponsored an expedition to the outer banks of present-day North Carolina, where Richard Grenville established a colony on Roanoke Island. Local Indians harrassed the settlers so relentlessly that the colony was abandoned within a year.

Raleigh tried again in 1587, sending 117 settlers to Roanoke under the leadership of Governor John White. At Roanoke colony Grenville's daughter gave birth to Virginia Dare, the first person of English descent born in the New World. The settlers learned to eat potatoes, a new food that White took back to England when he returned for supplies. White

CRUISE TO DISASTER

During the age of exploration, the English nurtured a fascination with foreign countries and a curiosity to know more about them. Descriptions and captives brought back from Newfoundland in the first decades of the 16th century filled the English mind with exotic images of the New World. In 1536 a London leather merchant named Richard Hore decided to cash in on the general interest in Newfoundland and to do some fishing along the Grand Banks. Chartering two ships, he advertised a tourist cruise to the island. His "perswasions tooke such effect," wrote historian Richard Hakluyt, that he signed up "six score persons, whereof thirty were gentlemen" for the trip.

The party sailed in April 1536. One ship was lost on the way over, but the other reached America after two months. Stopping first at Penguin Island, the visitors hunted for great auk and bear. Hore then took his customers to Newfoundland. Probably because most of the passengers were unaccustomed to physical labor, the party was unable to feed itself by hunting and fishing. Their provisions dwindled and they took to robbing osprey nests for fish and gathering roots and leaves to eat. Because they had no supplies for another voyage, they could not return to England. As starvation set in, some of the party allegedly resorted to cannibalism, killing and eating their fellow tourists. When an unsuspecting French ship arrived, the Englishmen captured and looted it. With the provisions they stole, the survivors sailed back to England in October.

intended to sail back to Roanoke promptly, but he was delayed in England by the war against the Spanish Armada (naval fleet). When he again landed at Roanoke, in 1590, the colony had vanished. The mystery of the "Lost Colony" has never been solved.

In Maine, Gorges's North Virginia Company of Plymouth was equally unsuccessful. The company was attracted to the mouth of the Kennebec River by reports from George Weymouth, who visited the area in 1605. Weymouth described the area as a trader's dream, writing that one morning "I traded with the savages all the forenoon upon the shore, . . . where for knives, glasses, combs, and other trifles to the value of four or five shillings, we had forty good beavers' skins, otters' skins, sables, and other small skins, which we knew not how to call." Weymouth also met a Patuxet Indian by the name of Squanto, whom he found intelligent and helpful. The good news encouraged Gorges to send two ships and 120 men to the Kennebec in 1607 to establish a trading settlement. But the operation was not profitable and the company abandoned its project.

FROM SURVIVAL TO SLAVERY IN THE SOUTH

Until 1614, England's first successful permanent settlement hardly looked like a success. In 1606 the South Virginia Company of London sent three ships and 104 settlers to Virginia to found a colony. When they arrived at "the Bay of Chesupioc" in 1607, one of the settlers recorded his impression of the countryside: "wee descried the Land of Virginia: . . . faire meddowes and goodly tall Trees, with such Fresh-waters runninge through the woods as I was almost ravished at the first Sight thereof." The inviting land, however, would be much harder to live on than the settlers imagined. They did not know they had landed in the heart of the East Coast's largest and most concentrated Indian population. Two hundred villages dotted the Tidewater region from the Potomac River to Albemarle Sound; about 14,000 Indians lived between the Chesapeake Bay and the falls of the James River alone. United under a chief named Wahunsonacock (whom the English called Powhatan), the tribes formed a powerful confederacy.

Founding Jamestown on an uninhabited island in the James River, the settlers soon learned why no Indians lived there: Mosquitoes flourished in the surrounding water. Throughout the summer, the settlers battled malaria. Almost half of them were wealthy gentlemen who did not expect to work and were accompanied by their footmen. Instead of planting crops, most of the colonists spent the planting season hunting for gold. To feed themselves, they forced the Indians to sell them food, or they stole it outright. Over the winter many died of starvation and disease. By 1608 only 38 remained alive. Most of the English settlers who continued to arrive in Jamestown in the next few years died of hunger or disease as well.

Virginia's fortunes began to turn when the settlers learned how to plant tobacco. The first shipment reached England in 1614, sparking an enormous demand. Colonists spread through the countryside and started tobacco farms, while hundreds of newcomers flooded in to participate in the boom. Between 1619 and 1621, 3,570 settlers arrived in Virginia, hoping to turn Indian hunting grounds into plantations. All this took place with little regard for the Tidewater Indians.

In 1618 the conciliatory Powhatan died and was succeeded by his brother Opechancanough, who deeply resented white mistreatment. The new chief planned a campaign of retaliation and bided his time. In 1622, when the English executed an Indian for the suspected murder of a white trader, the Indians launched a bloody surprise attack. They killed 347 of Virginia's 1,200 white inhabitants and destroyed a number of outposts. The angry whites initiated a program of extermination and struck the Indians savagely, killing many and burning villages and crops. In a 1624 message to the South Virginia Company in London, they reported that

> We have to our uttermost abilities revenged ourselves upon the savages on this river, cut down their corn in all places. . . . Burning down the houses they have reedified, and with the slaughters of many have enforced them to abandon their plantations.

That year Virginia became a royal colony, and the company was disbanded. The massacre of Indians continued while the white population grew. Finally the English captured and killed Opechancanough in 1646. The Powhatan Confederacy was destroyed and Indian lands confiscated. Within 25 years, only 2,000 of the region's 30,000 Tidewater Indians were left.

By contrast, there were 32,000 English colonists in Virginia in 1674, and white settlement had spread westward to the Piedmont Plateau. Tensions between settlers and the Nanticoke and Susquehannock Indians soon erupted in violence. White and Indian attacks and counterattacks culminated in Nathaniel Bacon's 1676 vigilante raids. When Bacon led a massacre of peaceful Pamukey Indians, who had long been friendly with whites, Virginia Governor William Berkeley labeled him a traitor. In response, the vigilantes captured and burned Jamestown. Bacon died of disease soon afterward, and the rebellion ended. Berkeley dispersed the rebels and made peace with the battered Indians, which opened still more land to white settlement. As Indian resistance in Virginia was subdued and the tobacco industry flourished, many black slaves were brought into the colony.

By that time, Carolina Colony was just getting on its feet. Settlers had trickled down from Virginia to the Albemarle Sound in the 1650s, and in 1663 King Charles II had granted the colony to eight wealthy proprietors. Two widely separated areas of settlement developed independent of each other, one at Albemarle Sound (North Carolina) and the other at Charles Town (South Carolina). Few colonists went to North Carolina at first, and the colony had no permanent town until a group of dissident French Huguenots arrived in 1704. White advancement in the area ignited the Tuscarora War of 1711 to 1713, in which most of the tribe was wiped out. The surviving Tuscarora went north in 1722 and joined the Iroquois League. North Carolina did not become a royal colony until 1729.

South Carolina grew more rapidly. In 1669 three ships filled with 100 settlers sailed from London, stopping on the Caribbean island of Barbados to pick up more settlers. This group built Charles Town on the Ashley River. (In 1680 the town moved to its present location on Charleston Harbor.) For 20 years the colony made a meager living from the fur trade and by exporting Indian slaves to the West Indies. White enslavement of Indians often led to retaliatory violence. Still, South Carolina started to thrive with the introduction of rice as a cash crop in the 1690s. Spreading out over Indian lands to start rice plantations, colonists began importing black slaves. In 1715 Yamasee Indians resentful of white expansion started skirmishing with the colonists. Although South Carolina became a royal colony in 1719, the Yamasee conflict lasted until 1728.

In 1732 King George II chartered the last of the land-grant colonies. Seeing an opportunity to create a buffer between the prospering Carolinas and Spanish Florida, the king granted Georgia to a social reformer named James Oglethorpe, who wanted to establish a colony for England's poor. The next year Oglethorpe and 125 settlers founded the settlement of Savannah on the Savannah River. A group of Lutherans arrived from Salzburg, Austria in 1734 and established the independent settlement of New Ebenezer farther upriver. While the Salzburgers pursued an orderly, industrious life, the inhabitants of Savannah were restless and unruly. Many left the town to find their fortunes in the countryside, in the process bringing smallpox to the Cherokee. Although the colony's original charter banned slavery, rice planters smuggled slaves in and convinced the colony to lift the ban in 1750. In 1753 Georgia became a royal colony.

NEW NETHERLAND AND THE MIDDLE COLONIES

England faced some competition from Holland in the race to establish a presence in the mid-Atlantic region. In 1609 the Dutch East India Company sent Englishman Henry Hudson across the ocean to find a route to Asia. Instead of Asia, he found New York Harbor and sailed up the river that bears his name. Eager to gain a foothold in the fur trade, the Dutch started sending ships to the area almost immediately. In 1614 the United New Netherland Company set up a trading post on the southern tip of Manhattan Island. It soon enjoyed a brisk trade in furs along the Atlantic coast from Delaware Bay to the Connecticut River and out along Long Island.

At least initially, their single-minded interest in trade and lack of interest in farming motivated the Dutch to maintain peaceful relations with the Indians. Their policy was to extend trade through treaties with the tribes concerned. What little white displacement of Indians did occur involved small land acquisitions accomplished by negotiation. But after the Dutch West India Company replaced the United New Netherland Company in 1621, Dutch settlement started to inch up the Hudson River. In 1624 the company built Fort Orange (present-day Albany) as a base for trade with the Iroquois. The Dutch at Fort Orange traded guns for furs; as the supply of fur was depleted in Iroquois territory, the Iroquois used those guns against their French and Huron rivals. (See Chapter 4.) To secure the Dutch position against French and British threats, Governor Peter Minuit bought Manhattan Island from the Manhattan Indians in 1626 for goods worth 60 guilders ($24.00). A fort was built and the colony of New Amsterdam grew up around it.

Dutch-Indian relations became strained in the 1630s, when the Dutch began settling down as farmers. At the same time, the company lost its monopoly and independent Dutch traders arrived. The unsupervised traders began mistreating Indians. White-Indian violence broke out and only worsened in 1639, when an overtly anti-Indian governor, William Kieft, took over. A believer in Indian extermination, Kieft offered bounties for Indian scalps when fighting erupted on Staten Island in 1641.

The Dutch signed a treaty with the Mohawk, longtime enemies of the Wappinger Confederacy, when war broke out with the confederacy in 1643. Colonists massacred Indians and Indians raided settlements until 1647, when the confederacy was finally crushed. New Netherland reached a population of 2,000 in the early 1650s and continued to grow, resulting in several Indian wars between 1655 and 1660. When English ships sailed into New Amsterdam in 1664, the Dutch had neither the means nor the inclination to put up a fight. The duke of York claimed New Netherland and renamed it New York; Fort Orange was renamed Albany.

The duke divided New York among his friends, granting New Jersey to Sir George Carteret and Lord John Berkeley and Delaware to William Penn, the founder of Philadelphia. Delaware, meanwhile, had been claimed by Sweden in 1638, when Swedish traders built Fort Christina on the site of present-day Wilmington. A few hundred Swedish settlers had made their way along the Delaware River, building the first log cabins in North America. Although it enjoyed peaceful relations with the Indians, New Sweden lasted only to 1655, when the Dutch took possession. Penn gained the charter in 1682 and united Delaware with Pennsylvania. In 1701 Delaware separated from Pennsylvania and became a royal colony. The next year the English also took over thinly settled New Jersey.

In 1632 King Charles I granted 7 million acres (2.8 million hectares) north of the Potomac river to George Calvert, the first Lord Baltimore, to establish a colony of Catholic dissidents from Protestant England. Calvert, a Catholic convert, died soon after he received the grant. His son Cecilius Calvert took over the Maryland venture. Accompanied by 17 Catholic gentlemen and 100 mostly Protestant servants, the second Lord Baltimore arrived in Maryland in 1633. The dissidents established peaceful relations with the Nanticoke Indians, whose numbers had dwindled due to prior contact with whites. As Maryland grew, members of its social elite were granted manorial estates that they operated by recruiting tenant farmers or by importing slaves. Tobacco became the major cash crop. By 1676 Maryland had 60 manorial estates and numerous small farms owned by freeholders.

Another religious dissident received a land grant to the north. William Penn, a member of the Society of Friends (Quakers), asked King Charles II for permission to found a Quaker colony in North America. When the king granted him Pennsylvania in 1681, Penn sold plots of land to approximately 1,100 Quaker settlers, most of whom reached the colony before he did. Arriving in 1682, Penn founded Philadelphia and signed a treaty with the leaders of the Delaware Confederacy, confirming Indian title to the territory and outlining procedures for the sale of Indian land to whites. The Quaker respect for the rights of Indians allowed the settlers to live in harmony with the Delaware for about 50 years.

Pennsylvania grew rapidly. As white colonists pressed out into the countryside, Pennsylvania began to lose its Quaker identity, although Philadelphia remained a stronghold of Quaker merchants. In 1717 the first of many Scotch-Irish settlers arrived and headed for the frontier of white settlement along the Susquehanna River. Disregarding Penn's 1682 treaty, they moved illegally onto Indian land and squatted there. The Indians resisted selling their land, and in the 1730s disputes between whites and Indians occurred frequently. By 1751 white expansion forced the Delaware to move west of the Allegheny Mountains.

PURITAN COUNTRY

When the first English settlers started to look toward New England, Sir Ferdinando Gorges held the royal patent on the land there. In 1620 he was granted the territory between the 40th and 48th parallels, but it was not Gorges who settled New England. The first permanent English settlement in New England was founded by a group of Puritan religious dissenters who called themselves Pilgrims. In 1620, 102 Pilgrims arrived in the North American wilderness on a ship called the

Mayflower, reaching Plymouth on the day after Christmas. Because an epidemic of European disease had wiped out the Indians in the area, the Pilgrims found an empty land ripe for settlement.

Nearly half the Pilgrims died during that first winter in America. Conditions improved in the spring of 1621, when they met the Patuxet Indian named Squanto and a Wampanoag Indian named Samoset. Squanto had spent considerable time in England and had learned to speak the language. Hoping to promote white-Indian trade, Squanto and Samoset helped the Pilgrims negotiate a peace treaty with Wampanoag chief Massasoit. Squanto also taught the settlers survival skills, such as how to plant maize. That fall they celebrated a good harvest, holding a feast with the Indians that came to be known as the first Thanksgiving.

The Pilgrims were soon trading for furs with the Massachuset Indians. Gorges granted Plymouth Colony a patent, but the colony was far from secure. In 1622 the Puritans got word of the Indian massacre of settlers in Virginia. Other white outposts had grown up nearby, inhabited by non-Puritans whose mistreatment had provoked the Indians. Suspecting that the Indians were planning an attack, the Pilgrims prepared their defenses and launched a preemptive assault, killing seven.

The white population of Plymouth Colony reached 180 in 1624 and 300 in 1630. Another group of Puritans began arriving in 1628, when Gorges granted a tract of land north of Plymouth to a Puritan group called the New England Company. In 1629 the company reorganized as the Massachusetts Bay Company and received a charter from King Charles I to establish a self-governing colony. As many as 20,000 Puritans had arrived in the new colony by 1640, founding such towns as Boston, Roxbury, and Cambridge.

During this period, Puritans and dissidents from Plymouth and Massachusetts Bay started moving out into the countryside, going as far away as present-day Maine and New Hampshire. The Council for New England had granted that region to Gorges and Captain John Mason in 1622, and in 1629 the men had it divided between themselves. Settlement remained sparse, but the Puritans claimed the region belonged to them. Massachusetts Bay Colony took over New Hampshire in the early 1640s and Maine in the 1650s. New Hampshire became a royal colony in 1679, and Massachusetts bought Maine in 1691, the same year it absorbed Plymouth.

As they became more firmly established, Puritan authorities applied their strict moral laws not only to white settlers but to the Indians, punishing them for breaking rules they did not know existed. The Indians also suffered epidemics of disease spread by the settlers and were tricked into selling their land under the pretense that they would still be able to use it.

In 1635, when Roger Williams criticized the Puritan leadership for its spiritual and moral hypocrisy (including its treatment of the Indians), he was exiled from Massachusetts Bay Colony. Along with a group of Quakers and other dissidents, Williams moved south to Narragansett Bay and founded Providence Plantation. Among the colony's guiding principles was an ethic of fair treatment of the Indians. Williams's group was soon joined by other migrants to the area, who founded Rhode Island Plantation. The two groups consolidated in 1640, forming the colony of Providence and Rhode Island Plantations. Four years later the colony received a charter from the Puritan Parliament of Massachusetts Bay Colony.

Meanwhile, Puritans were moving from Massachusetts Bay to the Connecticut River area, which had been depopulated of Indians by epidemics. The first Puritans made the trip in 1633; they were joined by many more in 1635 and 1636. The Connecticut settlers hoped to clear the area of Pequot Indians who had survived the plagues. The Pequot, whom the Puritans believed were agents of Satan, angered the English by continuing trade with the Dutch.

When Indians killed two unscrupulous English traders, the colonists demanded that the guilty parties be turned in. The Indians refused and the whites attacked, igniting the Pequot War in 1636. The Connecticut settlers allied with the Mohegan, Narraganset, and Niantic and struck the Pequot with a ferocity that horrified their Indian allies. In 1637 the Puritans raided the main Pequot village. Setting fire to the compound, they burned many Indians to death and hacked down those trying to escape, killing at least 600. They then hunted down remaining bands of Pequot, killing as many as they could and sending the survivors to the West Indies as slaves. In the end, the Pequot were almost entirely wiped out.

Fighting between English and Dutch settlers in 17th-century Connecticut. (Picture Collection, The Branch Libraries, The New York Public Library)

The Pequot War heightened anti-Indian sentiment among most New England settlers, many of whom called the Indians devils. It seemed little could ease relations between New England's whites and Indians. After the war, a group of especially conservative Puritans left

New England colonists mount Metacom's head on a stake in 1676 after defeating him in King Philip's War. (Picture Collection, The Branch Libraries, The New York Public Library)

Massachusetts Bay Colony and in 1638 founded New Haven Colony to the west of Connecticut Colony, which separated from Massachusetts in 1639. The ongoing English influx forced the Dutch to surrender their trading post on the Connecticut River in 1653. In 1662 Connecticut became a royal colony and absorbed New Haven.

In 1675, 40,000 English settlers and 20,000 Indians lived between the Hudson and Kennebec rivers. White expansion threatened Indian security and led to frequent mistreatment of Indians. Tensions rose after Wampanoag chief Massasoit, who had worked to maintain peace with the Puritans, died in 1661. His son Metacom (whom the English called King Philip) was far less conciliatory. To counter the white threat, Metacom sent representatives to tribes throughout New England in an effort to promote intertribal unity.

In response to the 1675 arrest and execution of a Wampanoag for murdering a white settler, Metacom attacked Puritan outposts. His early victories encouraged other New England tribes to move against their English neighbors, while the colonists mobilized their militias and their Indian allies. In the large-scale conflict that came to be known as King Philip's War, the Indians attacked 52 of New England's 90 white settlements, burning some and completely obliterating two. Only Rhode Island was spared, because of its fair treatment of the Indians there.

After a year of vicious fighting, the Puritans captured and executed Metacom. The colonists exterminated many Indian survivors of the war and sold others—including Metacom's wife and son—as slaves. The English victory in King Philip's War essentially wiped out Indian resistance in New England. It also fixed the colonists' image of the Indian as an unredeemable savage unworthy of white tolerance. This attitude would be inherited by subsequent generations of white settlers and would form the basis of English and, ultimately, United States Indian policy.

TO THE NORTH

In the territory now occupied by Canada, England's chief rivals were not the Indians but the French. The English wanted a piece of the lucrative fur trade and of the riches harvested by fishing boats in northern Atlantic waters. Sailing for the Dutch in 1610, Henry Hudson had explored Hudson Bay and its southern extension, James Bay. England sent several subsequent expeditions to the area.

In 1615 and 1616 Robert Bylot and William Baffin made two voyages, sailing through Davis Strait to Baffin Bay and locating Lancaster Sound. The explorers returned to England without realizing they had discovered the entrance to the much sought-after Northwest Passage. Thomas James and Luke Fox continued the English investigation in 1631, probing the shores of James Bay. It was on those shores that the English fur-trading concern called the Hudson's Bay Company built its first trading post in 1670. Hudson's Bay agents soon spread south and west, making contact with Indian trappers and diverting some of the fur trade away from the French. The competition for the fur trade would soon become a cause for war among the English, the French, and the Indians.

Along the Atlantic coast, England focused on fishing and agriculture. The waters there swarmed with cod and other fish as well as with

Eighteenth-century fishermen process their catch of cod on the shores of Newfoundland.
(Picture Collection, The Branch Libraries, The New York Public Library)

oil-bearing whales, walruses, and seals. In 1610 a group of investors organized the London and Bristol Company for the Colonization of Newfoundland to establish a fishing colony on that island. The crown granted Newfoundland to the company, and John Guy led 40 colonists over to start the venture. Unable to feed themselves in the harsh environment, the settlers required frequent provisioning from England. The colony proved unprofitable, and only a few British settlers lived on Newfoundland during the 17th century.

Hoping to establish a buffer between New England and New France, King James I granted Nova Scotia (New Scotland) to a Scotsman named Sir William Alexander in 1621, ignoring France's claim on the region it called Acadia. But few Scots were willing to invest in the settlement of the disputed territory, even after King Charles I designated it part of the Scottish Kingdom.

When war broke out between England and France in 1627, three brothers—David, Louis, and Thomas Kirke—sailed to the St. Lawrence River under the auspices of the recently chartered English Canada Company. They built a base at Tadoussac, captured a French fleet commanded by Samuel de Champlain, and demanded that Champlain surrender. At the same time, Scottish settlers occupied Port Royal, Nova Scotia, which Champlain had abandoned. In 1629, when Champlain surrendered, England claimed New France and Acadia. But the crown was desperate for money, and in 1632 Charles I signed the Treaty of St. Germain-en-Laye, returning the captured territory to France in exchange for 400,000 crowns. In 1654 England once again took Acadia, but diplomatic wrangling in Europe returned it to France in 1671. The real struggle for North America was still to come.

CHAPTER FIVE NOTES

p. 58   "... our chiefe desire ..." Quoted in J. Bartlet Brebner. *Canada*, new ed., rev. and enlarged by Donald C. Masters (Ann Arbor, MI: University of Michigan Press, 1970), p. 23.

p. 60   "perswasions tooke ..." Quoted in Samuel Eliot Morison. *The European Discovery of America: The Northern Voyages* (New York: Oxford University Press, 1971), p. 237.

p. 61   "I traded with the ..." Quoted in Debo. p. 39.

p. 61   "... wee descried the land ..." Quoted in Debo. p. 39.

p. 62   "We have to our uttermost ..." Quoted in Morgan. p. 131.

CONTEST FOR A CONTINENT

The same objectives that brought Europeans to North America in the first place brought them into conflict with each other once they arrived. From late in the 17th century into the 19th century, the three main European powers in the New World—Spain, France, and England—struggled for control of its resources and potential. Much of the time this struggle paralleled wars in Europe, with North America serving as but one arena in which European rivalries were played out. The separate concerns of those who lived in the New World added another dimension to the fighting, as Indians resisted the incursion of white settlers or battled for control of trade with them. At the same time, the white settlers began to think of themselves as Americans or Canadians, people whose interests differed from or even ran counter to those of Europeans.

North America was thus a battlefield throughout the 18th century, its many wars seeming to flow into one long war punctuated by occasional periods of truce. For many decades the main combatants were England and France, because Spain's holdings north of Mexico were relatively remote. Spain did play a role, however, largely as an ally of France. Louisiana and New France also benefited from the many

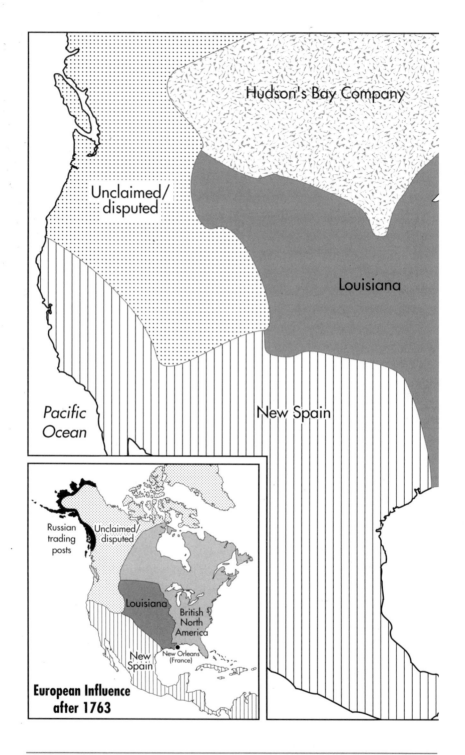

Hudson's Bay Company

Unclaimed/
disputed

Louisiana

Pacific
Ocean

New Spain

Russian
trading
posts

Unclaimed/
disputed

Louisiana

British
North
America

New
Spain

New Orleans
(France)

**European Influence
after 1763**

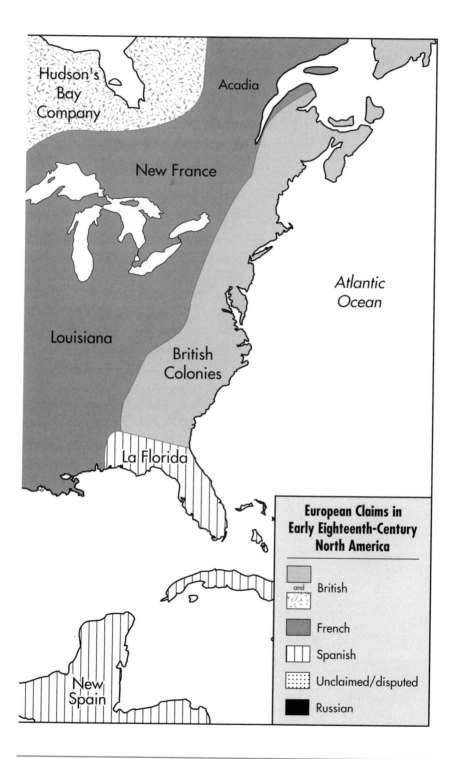

European Claims in Early Eighteenth-Century North America

British

French

Spanish

Unclaimed/disputed

Russian

French alliances with Indian tribes and from its proud military tradition. From 1669 on New France maintained a militia composed of all its male colonists between the ages of 16 and 60. This militia was not called into action until 1684, but thereafter it was used steadily until 1760. Its frequent successes against the more numerous English forces had much to do with Canadian settlers' knowledge of Indian guerrilla tactics. The English crown relied on English soldiers and traditional European military techniques to defend its colonies, but American settlers picked up Indian war tactics and used them to great effect against English soldiers, French settlers, and the Indians themselves.

THE IMPERIAL WARS

The first full-scale confrontation between the imperial powers in North America was King William's War (1689–97). From 1665 on the rapid westward expansion of the French fur trade, Iroquois loyalty to the English, and English intrusion into previously French territory sparked hostilities that soon included the Abnaki Indians, who allied with France. Tensions between the French and English settlers had reached the boiling point by 1689, when the War of the League of Augsburg (the War of the Palatinate) broke out in Europe. That conflict pitted England and the Netherlands against France and spilled over into the New World, where it was known as King William's War. After repeated skirmishes with the Iroquois, the French attempted to make peace but were rebuffed, for the Iroquois felt confident they could crush New France with backing from the large English army.

The swashbuckling French, of course, saw things differently. They considered the settled, industrious colonists of New England weak and timid. One French military officer voiced this opinion after a visit to the English colonies:

> It is true that this country has twice the population of New France, but the people there are astonishingly cowardly, completely undisciplined, and without any experience in war. The smallest Indian party has always made them flee, moreover, they have no regular troops. . . . the Canadians are brave, much inured to war, and untiring in travel; two thousand of them will at all times and in all places thrash the people of New England.

Fired by that same confidence, New France Governor Louis de Baude de Frontenac ordered a three-pronged push into English territory in 1690. The attack left 60 English settlers dead at Schenectady, New York, 34 dead at Salmon Falls, New Hampshire, and more than 100 dead at Fort Loyal (Falmouth), Maine. Under Sir William Phipps, the English navy took Port Royal, the center of Acadia's population of less than 1,000, but British forces were deflected at Quebec. Pierre Le Moyne, sieur d'Iberville, commanded France's naval counterstrike, leading three ships in an unsuccessful attack on the English at Hudson's Bay.

With an army of 300, Englishman Benjamin Church attacked the Abnaki Indians in 1691. The next year the Abnaki and their French allies killed 48 English settlers and captured 70 at York, Maine. Iberville continued his naval campaign in 1694, capturing Fort York on Hudson's Bay and renaming it Fort Bourbon. When England's Iroquois allies reached a truce with France's Ottawa Indian trading partners, the French saw the agreement as a threat and destroyed the villages of the Onondaga and Oneida Iroquois. Meanwhile, the French and English continued to raid each other's settlements. Finally in 1697 the Treaty of Ryswyck ended the war in Europe and returned Acadia to France. Still, the French kept up military pressure on the Iroquois in order to minimize their interference in the fur trade. The strategy paid off in 1701, when all the Iroquois tribes agreed not to interfere with French trading activity. A great victory for the French, the Iroquois pledge of neutrality was a terrible blow to English fur traders.

While French and English traders fought for control of the fur trade around Hudson's Bay (in an area the English called Rupert's Land), imperial politics produced an alliance between France and Spain in 1700; from that point onward the two powers cooperated in North America. The formation of this new alliance ignited Europe's War of the Spanish Succession in 1702. Referred to as Queen Anne's War (1702–13) in America, the conflict united England, Austria, and the Netherlands against France and Spain. A border war immediately broke out between English South Carolina and Spanish Florida. British ships sacked the Spanish settlement of St. Augustine, while on land the English assaulted Spanish missions among the Apalachee Indians of west Florida. In the raids, the English killed many Apalachee and captured almost all the survivors, virtually destroying that culture.

Elsewhere in the south, the Choctaw and Creek sided with the French, the Chickasaw sided with the English, and the Cherokee remained neutral.

To the north, the French joined forces with their Abnaki allies to attack settlements in New England. The English launched their own counterraids and tried to enlist Iroquois aid. Although angered by French abuses—particularly the establishment of a settlement at Detroit—the Iroquois remained neutral. A British naval attempt to take Port Royal failed in 1707, but in 1710 reinforcements arrived from England and the Nova Scotia post fell. But the English still could not capture Quebec. A 1711 naval campaign was shipwrecked at the mouth of the St. Lawrence River, leaving 1,600 sailors dead.

A year later the war in Europe ended. Under the Treaty of Utrecht (1713), France's King Louis XIV recognized English "sovereignty" over the Iroquois and ceded Hudson's Bay and most of Acadia to England. France was allowed to keep Île-Royale (now Cape Breton Island) and Île-Saint-Jean (now Prince Edward Island), and it soon became clear that France had not given up on Acadia. Building a fortified seaport at Louisbourg on Île-Royale, the French established a thriving settlement that grew rapidly, reaching a population of 2,600 in the 1740s. Louisbourg's military garrison was poorly managed and provisioned, but the large French presence just to the north made New Englanders nervous.

The English worried with reason, for their population in Acadia grew slowly while the French and Indian populations remained large. In 1725 the English were forced to sign a treaty that allowed the Micmac Indians to live in their own territory on Nova Scotia. Determined to remove the Acadians, as the French inhabitants of the region were known, the English gave them one year to vacate the area or become English subjects. Almost none of the Acadians left, and although Catholicism was illegal under British law, they continued to practice their religion and speak French. The British had to compromise with the stubborn Acadians in the 1720s, when they refused to swear oaths of allegiance to the British crown.

England also had problems with the Spanish in the New World. In 1733 Spain established Florida as a refuge for black slaves who escaped from Britain's Carolina colonies. Enough slaves escaped to

Florida—where they were declared free—that the English began to worry. By 1738, 80 freed slaves lived in St. Augustine. The Spanish population also grew large enough to be of concern: In 1740 about 3,000 Spanish colonists lived in Florida. The English laid siege to St. Augustine that year, but after 38 days failed to take the fort and abandoned the effort.

By 1743 France and Prussia had started fighting England and Austria in the War of the Austrian Succession, known as King George's War (1744–48) in the colonies. Fort St. Frederick on Lake Champlain served as a base for French and Indian raids on New York and New England, while in Acadia French forces based at Louisbourg tried but failed to capture Port Royal. In 1745 William Pepperell led 4,200 New Englanders to Louisbourg and captured the fort after a two-month siege. Although successful, the unauthorized operation was hardly an example of military efficiency. One observer on the scene wrote that the American ranks

indeed presented a formidable front to the enemy, but the rear was a scene of confusion and frolic. While some were on duty . . . others were racing, wrestling, pitching quoits, firing at marks or at birds, or running after shot from the enemy's guns, for which they received a bounty.

The balance of power continued to shift back and forth in North America. The French launched a series of major attacks on English settlements in New York, New Hampshire, and Massachusetts. In the process, many English captives were taken to New France. An Irish fur trader and land speculator named William Johnson convinced the Mohawk to end their neutrality and led them in an attack on Fort St. Frederick, but the French there could not be overcome. In the south the Cherokee also took the side of the English and fought alongside the Chickasaw against the pro-French Choctaw and Creek, seriously disrupting French trade along the Mississippi. The skirmishing ended when the war in Europe drew to a close in 1748. France and England signed the Treaty of Aix-la-Chapelle, which among other things returned Louisbourg to France in exchange for French-held Madras in India.

Not surprisingly, the treaty did not solve the North American problem. To counterbalance the French presence at Louisbourg, the British founded Halifax, Nova Scotia in 1749. They hoped the settlement would encourage English migration to the territory, but the immigrants who came often had no skills or motivation. The British tried to improve the caliber of the population by recruiting French Huguenots and Swiss and German immigrants. But these settlers were disgruntled that they could not gain title to farmland still occupied by Acadians. At the same time, English problems with the Micmac persisted. When the Indians declared war on the settlers, the English authorities offered a bounty on Micmac scalps. The policy led to the death of many Indians, the flight of many others, and the subjugation of the few survivors who remained in English territory.

Elsewhere in North America, French and English exploration and settlement steadily pushed colonial frontiers toward a collision. By 1750 the population of the English colonies reached 1.5 million. In the Ohio River Valley, which the Iroquois claimed during the 1740s, the English dominated the fur trade. Before long England asserted its rights to the region, and in 1749 it granted large tracts of land to the Ohio Company of Virginia. Under the company's auspices, English settlers began to arrive, enraging France, which insisted it owned the valley. In 1752 French, Ottawa, and Ojibwa forces attacked the English. Although backed by the Miami Indians, the English were routed.

After the victory, New France Governor Ange de Menneville, marquis de Duquesne, ordered 2,200 militiamen and Indians to the Ohio valley to build forts from Lake Erie to the Forks of the Ohio (the place where the Ohio, Allegheny, and Monongahela rivers meet, now the site of Pittsburgh, Pennsylvania). Although many Frenchmen died of disease in the effort, Duquesne managed to establish a grip on the area that lasted until 1758. Witnessing the shift of power in the area, Indian tribes such as the Ottawa, Algonkin, Wyandot, Nipissing, Ojibwa, Potawatomi, Sauk, Shawnee, Seneca, and Delaware allied themselves with the French.

The final showdown between France and England in North America was the French and Indian War (1754–63). Defying the French, the English started building a fort at the Forks of the Ohio in 1754. The English were able to persuade the Mingo Indians to

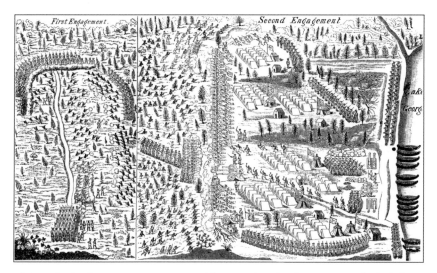

The Battle of Lake George (1755), part of the French and Indian War, in which William Johnson's Iroquois army defeated the French. (Picture Collection, The Branch Libraries, The New York Public Library)

ally with them, but the French evicted the English from their construction site and named it Fort Duquesne. William Johnson continued his campaign to convince the Iroquois to join forces with the English. Although he already had Mohawk support, some Iroquois were not enthusiastic about an English alliance. In a statement circulated among the Indians, a group of pro-French Catholic Iroquois warned of the dangers posed by the English:

> Brethren, are you ignorant of the difference between our Father and the English? Go see the forts our Father has erected, and you will see that the land beneath his walls is still hunting ground, having fixed himself in those places we frequent, only to supply our wants; whilst the English, on the contrary, no sooner get possession of a country than the game is forced to leave it; the trees fall down before them, the earth becomes bare, and we find among them hardly wherewithal to shelter us when the night falls.

The warning fell on deaf ears, and most Iroquois as well as tribes such as the Miami, Shawnee, and Delaware decided to ally with the English.

In 1755 Johnson led his Mohawk force against Fort St. Frederick. The French repelled the attack with the help of their own Indian allies, who included some Iroquois. Britain again demanded that the French Acadians take an oath of allegiance to the crown, but again the Acadians resisted. The English informed the Acadians that they were to be deported to French territory and then shipped them to New England and the other British colonies. Some English colonists reluctantly accepted the strangers, but others turned the ships away, forcing them to return to Nova Scotia. Among the Acadians who escaped deportation or returned to Nova Scotia, more than 2,000 migrated to Île-St.-Jean in the winter of 1755–56.

As the French and Indian War continued in North America, the Seven Years' War (1755–63) broke out in Europe, pitting England and Prussia against France, Spain, Austria, and Russia. The war in Europe intensified the fighting in the colonies. French and Indian forces gained the upper hand first, attacking and destroying English settlements along the Allegheny Mountain range and capturing several English posts. But by 1758 disagreements within the French command, epidemics among the soldiers and settlers, and a devastating crop failure weakened New France. At the same time, the colony's amateur militia was proving insufficient to the task of serious war-making. Colonel Louis-Antoine Bougainville wrote that the militiamen frequently "become disgusted; they wish to return home, to sow and to harvest; soon they declare themselves sick. Either they must be sent home or they become deserters . . . there is among the militia men no order and no submission."

British war minister William Pitt took advantage of the situation to take Louisbourg. Freed of the French threat in Acadia, English authorities initiated a program of French deportation known as the Acadian Expulsion. More than 6,000 Acadians were removed to France, while only 1,400 remained on Nova Scotia and accepted British rule. A number of Acadians managed to flee to the French territory of Louisiana and made their way to the bayous of the Mississippi River delta. Their descendants came to be known as Cajuns.

The English also blockaded Atlantic shipping lanes and captured many land positions held by the French. General John Forbes took Fort Duquesne and renamed it Fort Pitt, while repeated raids on

Quebec in 1759, just before it fell to the British. (Phelps Stokes Collection, The New York Public Library)

Quebec laid ruin to many settlements. The decisive blow came in 1760. That year General James Wolfe and Vice Admiral Sir Charles Saunders led 22,100 British soldiers and 119 ships to Quebec. After two months of fighting, the English captured Quebec City, then moved on to Montreal and in the Battle of the Plains of Abraham forced its surrender. These two English victories spelled the end of French power in North America.

No longer dependent on the Indians as military allies, the English set up a system of stringent regulations and harsh punishments for the Indian population of the Great Lakes and Ohio valley, a combined region called the Old Northwest. They stopped delivering supplies to the Indians and unceremoniously pushed them off their land. As Indian resentments multiplied, an Ottawa chief named Pontiac called for intertribal unity in the Old Northwest. Another Indian known as the Delaware Prophet, or Neolin, simultaneously preached in favor of a return to traditional ways. The Indians of the region embraced the messages of Pontiac and the Delaware Prophet and united with each other and with French settlers angered by English domination.

In 1763 Pontiac organized two attempts to capture the English fort at Detroit, both of which failed. He then laid siege to the fort and, joined by other tribes, attacked white settlements and forts throughout the Old Northwest. The Indians captured a number of English forts and killed 2,000 settlers, but Detroit remained impregnable. Then the Seven Years' War ended in Europe. The European powers signed the Treaty of Paris, leaving Pontiac's rebellion without French support. Pontiac wisely decided to end the siege of Detroit.

Under the Treaty of Paris, France ceded New France and all land east of the Mississippi River to England, while England ceded the Caribbean islands of Guadeloupe and Martinique to France. France also gave up Louisiana west of the Mississippi (except New Orleans) to its ally Spain, as compensation for Spain's loss of Florida to England. Many French-speaking Catholics remained in British North America, but England now controlled the entire eastern portion of the continent.

Formally establishing the Colony of Quebec, Britain tried to organize an effective colonial government there. The colony was of particular concern because its French Catholic population greatly outnumbered its English Protestant population. Designed to forestall potential conflicts, the Quebec Act of 1774 allowed the colony's French citizens to retain their language, religion, and court system. Meanwhile, more than 8,000 New Englanders were recruited to settle Nova Scotia, which now included New Brunswick as well as Cape Breton and Prince Edward islands. Half these recruits abandoned Nova Scotia within a few years, though, because the farmland was not as rich as New England soil and the colonial government did not allow them the independence they had enjoyed to the south.

THE AMERICAN REVOLUTION

By the mid-18th century, England's colonists in America had begun thinking of themselves as Americans rather than as English subjects. They resented British control over their lives and often disobeyed royal or parliamentary edicts. One such edict was the Royal Proclamation of 1763, which prohibited white settlement west of the crest of the Appalachian Mountains. American settlers ignored it and started migrating to the Old Northwest.

Late in the 1760s, the Iroquois and Cherokee finally gave up their claims to the Ohio valley. The Shawnee, however, resisted. When Virginia's governor, the earl of Dunmore, granted Shawnee land to veterans who had served under him in the French and Indian War, the Shawnee attacked. In 1774, 1,500 soldiers arrived to protect the white settlers. The Shawnee launched a surprise attack near Fort Pitt, killing 50 whites. But the Indians suffered heavy losses and were forced to surrender.

To the south, settlers in the Carolinas formed "Regulator" societies to keep Indians off land claimed by whites. In part because of pressure from the Regulators, the Cherokee agreed in 1770 to move the boundary of white settlement farther west. Colonization continued its westward advance in 1775, when a North Carolina judge named Richard Henderson bought portions of present-day Kentucky and Tennessee from the Cherokee. Explored by Daniel Boone, the region became a county of Virginia.

Meanwhile, tensions built between the American colonists and their British rulers. Many of the colonists did not want the British army on American soil and viewed Parliament as a tyrannical body with no right to rule them. Americans wrote defiant pamphlets, essays, and newspaper editorials and staged demonstrations, assaulted British officials, boycotted English imports, and formed organizations such as the Sons of Liberty. The resentment of British rule unified the previously divisive colonists behind a common cause.

Before long, violence erupted. In 1770 British soldiers taunted by a crowd in Boston opened fire, killing five Americans and wounding eight in the Boston Massacre. Ethan Allen's Green Mountain Boys fought the colonial governments of New York and New Hampshire to carve out an independent area called Vermont. In 1771 North Carolina Governor William Tryon led a militia against Regulators who snubbed British authority in the Piedmont, defeating the rebels at the Battle of Alamance. The British Tea Act of 1773 sparked the Boston Tea Party, leading to a British crackdown on the unruly colonists.

In 1774 representatives from the various colonies met in Philadelphia and issued a Declaration of American Rights, which Britain ignored. A year later the American Revolution erupted at the battles of Lexington and Concord. The Second Continental Congress

DEBORAH SAMPSON, PATRIOT

A free African-American from Plymouth, Massachusetts, Deborah Sampson (1760–1827) was inspired by intense patriotism to fight for independence during the American Revolution. She grew up working as a domestic servant and attended school part time, where she learned to read. Curious about politics, she followed the war closely in the newspapers. In 1778 she decided to do something for her country. She secretly sewed a man's suit and adopted the alias Robert Shurtleff, then walked to a nearby town in her new clothes and enlisted in the Continental Army.

Sampson's unusual height and stamina allowed her to conceal her gender while serving in the Fourth Regiment, even after she was wounded in the Battle of Tarrytown. She extracted musket balls from her own leg and returned to duty, then was shot in the shoulder at the Battle of Yorktown. But it was not until she came down with "brain fever" near Philadelphia that a doctor discovered her sex. Although the doctor kept her secret, Sampson was soon discharged from the army because of poor health. When her adventures came to light she went on the lecture circuit. With the help of Paul Revere, she secured a soldier's pension from the State of Massachusetts and from the federal government.

convened in Philadelphia to draft a Declaration of Independence, which was signed on July 4, 1776. The Congress formed a government and organized a military under a commander-in-chief named George Washington.

Both the British and the Americans sought help from the Indians during the war. Viewing the American settlers as the main threat to their land, most of the Indians sided with the British, whom they believed would enforce the Proclamation of 1763. In 1776 the Cherokee attacked American settlements in Virginia, the Carolinas, and Georgia. American militias retaliated, forcing the Indians to give

Lord Cornwallis surrenders to General Washington at the end of the American Revolution. (Picture Collection, The Branch Libraries, The New York Public Library)

up their land in 1777. Among the Iroquois, the Mohawk, Onondaga, Cayuga, and Seneca allied with the British and the Oneida and Tuscarora with the Americans. The white conflict thus forced the Iroquois to fight each other, leading to civil war and weakening the federation.

Throughout the war, many Americans died in British-Indian raids and many Indian villages were destroyed by the settlers. Indians were pivotal in the results of many confrontations between the British and the Americans. Still feuding with England, France took America's side in the conflict and sent military aid to the rebels. In the last battle of the war, Washington marched on the British at Yorktown, Virginia with French commander Jean-Baptiste-Donatien de Vimeur, comte de Rochambeau, while a French navy fleet sailed on the position. The allies trapped Lord Charles Cornwallis and the British surrendered in 1781.

Britain and the newly independent Confederate States of America formally ended the American Revolution in 1783, signing the Treaty of Paris. The treaty made no mention of the Indians who had done so much to help both sides. Some Indians were welcomed in British North

America (present-day Canada), but the American founders all but ignored them. The raiding and counterraiding of the war had turned whites and Indians into lasting enemies; from 1783 to 1790 at least 1,500 white Americans were killed in Indian attacks.

The war also pushed many tribes into the Old Northwest, a region now occupied by the states of Ohio, Indiana, Michigan, Illinois, Wisconsin, and the northeast corner of Minnesota. The Iroquois gave up most of western New York and Pennsylvania; the Cherokee relinquished their claims in the Carolinas, Tennessee, and Kentucky; fighting in Georgia pushed back the Creek border; in 1785 the tribes living in the Ohio valley ceded that land. Congress passed three ordinances, including the Northwest Ordinance of 1787, that established the Northwest Territory and laid out the means whereby it would be absorbed into the United States. It also drafted the Constitution of the United States of America in 1787, which was ratified by all 13 states by 1790.

THE FAR WEST

Aside from Florida, which England returned to Spain in 1783, all North American territory east of the Mississippi River and south of the Great Lakes belonged to the United States in 1800. West of the Mississippi, however, the contest for empire continued. The Pacific Northwest, from California to Alaska, was a focus of European activity throughout the 18th century. In 1732 Russian exploration of the Bering Sea commenced, and in 1741 Vitus Bering (a Dane working for Russia) sailed from Russia to Alaska across the Bering Strait.

The Russians engaged in an active trade in sea otter pelts with the indigenous Alaskans, and in 1783 they founded the first permanent Russian settlement in North America, on Kodiak Island. The Russian traders at the settlement and at other trading posts treated the Inuit with extreme cruelty. Other Europeans became interested in the lucrative fur trade and sent explorers to the area. The Spanish sailed up the Pacific coast from California, as did the English and the French. Adventurers such as Alexander Mackenzie made the overland trek across the continent.

To the south, Spanish exploration of the Southwest continued. Spain established its first Catholic mission in Texas in 1689; by 1718

Texas boasted the town of San Antonio, the chapel known as the Alamo, and three additional missions. In 1740 the Spanish population of New Mexico reached 5,000. Still, Spain worried about the arrival of Russian explorers and traders along the Pacific coast. To secure its claim to California, Spain sent a colonizing expedition to California in 1769. There the missionary named Fray Junípero Serra founded San Diego while Spanish soldiers and missionaries moved up the coast as far as San Francisco Bay.

In the long run, though, the most significant impact the Spanish had on North America was the introduction of the horse to the Indian tribes of the Great Plains and the Great Basin. As horses spread north from Mexico via trade, theft, and escape, the Indians adapted them for hunting and transportation. The mobility of nomadic tribes increased, while some settled village tribes became migratory hunters. The buffalo became the basis of the region's Indian economy. The increased intertribal contact that came from horse trading and wider travel allowed different tribes to pick up cultural traits and values from each other. Eventually the Great Plains tribes seemed to blend into a kind of "composite tribe" encountered by American pioneers in their 19th-century push to the west.

CHAPTER SIX NOTES

p. 78   "It is true . . ." Quoted in Eccles. p. 132.

p. 81   ". . . indeed presented a . . ." Quoted in Bumsted. p. 116.

p. 83   "Brethren, are you . . ." Quoted in Eccles. p. 158.

p. 84   ". . . become disgusted . . ." Quoted in Bumsted. p. 89.

COLONIALISM AND CONFEDERATION IN CANADA

Britain's defeat in the American Revolution redefined British North America. At the end of the 18th century, the region encompassed virtually all the territory north of the Great Lakes and the St. Lawrence River. Farther west, the division between United States and British territory was less clear. What was clear was the uncertainty facing French Canadians in the wake of Britain's eviction of France from North America in the French and Indian War. French migration slowed considerably, and people of French descent concentrated in the area now known as Quebec. British settlers, meanwhile, started streaming into the colonies, seeking economic opportunity as farmers, traders, and merchants. British North America would remain much more sparsely populated than the United States, but the extensive travels of fur traders employed by the North West Company and the Hudson's Bay Company allowed Britain to lay claim to huge stretches of the northern and western portions of present-day Canada.

Because of the relatively small numbers of whites in the region, settlement of the northern half of the continent would involve far less Indian bloodshed than did settlement of the southern half. At least initially, Canadians were more interested in trading with Indians than in displacing them; the moderate rate at which whites claimed farmland and forest permitted a relatively organized approach to conquest. Colonial authorities often designated Indian reserves before white settlers arrived, so the boundaries between whites and Indians were more clearly drawn than in the United States. Nevertheless, in the 19th century small-scale fighting broke out periodically, and epidemics of European disease killed many Indians on the Canadian plains and prairies as well as along the Pacific coast and in the Arctic. And although

THE LOYALISTS

Most of the loyalist migrants to British North America settled first in Nova Scotia, although many traveled to northern Quebec (present-day Ontario) instead. They founded Port Roseway (present-day Shelburne) on the peninsula of Nova Scotia, Saint John in present-day New Brunswick, and Cataraqui (present-day Kingston) on the shores of Lake Ontario. Largely farmers, tradespeople, and unskilled laborers, the loyalists came prepared to work for a living. Drawn by the lure of free land, they often faced a long and frustrating wait to receive it. Some, such as the Indians and the women, got no land at all, while the colonial government fulfilled its promise to fewer than half the black loyalists. The problems sparked some grumbling, but the land-grant program served to establish the Canadian policy of freeholding, in which individual settlers owned and worked small parcels of land.

Accustomed to town meetings and other democratic customs, these former Americans demanded a greater voice in unhurried, white advancement eventually robbed Indians of their ancestral homes. Between 1850 and 1923, Indians signed 16 treaties that ceded vast territories to Britain and Canada. They signed the treaties thinking they would still be able to hunt and fish on the land they gave up, but they soon learned they would be confined to reserves (reservations).

THE BRITISH INVASION

As soon as the American Revolution ended, the French and Indian inhabitants of British North America saw their old way of life give way before waves of British immigrants. The first to arrive were 40,000 British loyalists from the United States. These were either civilians who had stood by the crown during the Revolution or soldiers who had served in the British army. Among them were 2,000 of the countless

government than England intended to allow in its remaining colonies. Some loyalists even contended that they should be granted a separate province where they could carry on their American traditions. Those who had enjoyed wealth and power before the Revolution expected to retain their social position and insisted the government give them larger land grants. They claimed the privilege would be "highly Advantageous in diffusing and supporting a Spirit of Attachement to the British Constitution," but their humbler counterparts protested that such a practice would result in "a total exclusion of themselves and Familys, who if they became Settlers must either content themselves with barren or remote lands. Or submit to be Tenants to those, most of whom they consider their superiors in nothing but deeper Art and keener Policy."

In the end, the elite got its way and received more and better land than most of the other loyalist immigrants. Thus was born a two-tiered social, economic, and political system in British North America. Conflicts between the elite and the masses would determine the course of the region's political history for at least the next 80 years.

Indians who had assisted British forces and 3,000 former slaves who had fought for the crown in exchange for freedom. In dire need of colonists to till the soil and build the economy, the colonial government of British North America actively recruited the loyalists.

The first group of loyalists reached Nova Scotia in 1782. Six fleets of ships carrying loyalist passengers sailed from the United States to British North America in 1783, and smaller numbers filtered in until 1786. During the 1780s, the loyalists moved constantly from one farm or settlement to another in search of a better life. This ceaseless motion would characterize white settlers in 19th-century British North America as they relentlessly spread out across the continent.

By 1791 the white population of British North America topped 250,000. Approximately 140,000 of these colonists were of French extraction, and 110,000 claimed British or American roots. In addition, about 50,000 Indians lived in areas that had been settled by whites (areas north and east of the Great Lakes). That year colonial reorganization by the British Parliament yielded the Constitutional Act of 1791, which split Quebec into two colonies: predominantly French Lower Canada (present-day Quebec) and predominantly English Upper Canada (present-day Ontario). Each colony was allowed to elect a representative assembly to govern in conjunction with the executive and legislative councils made up of colonial administrators. The two-tiered government, made up of elite appointees and popularly elected representatives, hastened the division of colonial society into two strata. This class division solidified along economic lines.

The economy of British North America developed through the exploitation of its abundant natural resources. Fishing tapped the seas and agriculture (especially grain farming) tapped the soil. Fur trapping dwindled steadily, but settlers learned to harvest another forest resource: timber. Commerce and manufacturing helped towns and cities grow, and the importance of Indians to the economy was recognized in the Jay Treaty of 1794, which permitted Mohawk traders to travel freely between British North America and the United States.

CONFRONTATION IN RUPERT'S LAND

At the dawn of the 19th century, an enormous portion of present-day Canada belonged to a fur-trading concern, the Hudson's

Bay Company. Known as Rupert's Land, the company's holdings encompassed the Ungava Peninsula in present-day Quebec as well as present-day Manitoba, Alberta, Saskatchewan, Northwest Territories, and Yukon Territory. In 1790 Spain had signed the Nootka Convention, in which it forfeited its claims in the Pacific Northwest to Britain and the United States. Through the activities of fur traders from the Hudson's Bay Company and its rival, the North West Company, Britain strengthened its claims to all the land between Hudson Bay and the Pacific Ocean. From 1790 to 1840 the fur trade represented a relatively small component of the British North American economy, but exploration by fur traders was essential to white settlement.

Although the territory technically belonged to the Hudson's Bay Company, the North West Company dominated the Montreal-based fur trade in Rupert's Land. Its employees completed many overland trips from Montreal to the Pacific coast, opening the area to white exploitation. The company monopolized the British fur trade along the Pacific coast, but in the interior it faced serious competition from the Hudson's Bay Company. Viewing the North West Company as an interloper in its territory and a drain on its profits, the Hudson's Bay Company decided to take action on the prairies in 1811.

In Scotland, Lord Thomas Douglas, the fifth earl of Selkirk, and his family had gained control of a large share of the Hudson's Bay Company. The company granted him a 116,000-square-mile (255,500-square-kilometer) portion of Rupert's Land that included parts of present-day Manitoba, North Dakota, and Minnesota. Naming the territory Assiniboia for the Assiniboine Indians who lived there, Selkirk selected a site at the junction of the Assiniboine and Red rivers (the approximate location of present-day Winnipeg) for a settlement. Under Miles Macdonnell, whom he named governor of Assiniboia, Selkirk sent a party of Scottish Highlanders to the site in 1812. There they built Fort Douglas.

The arrival of Selkirk's colonists caused immediate tensions in the area. Not only was the North West Company disgruntled at the intrusion of farmers sent into fur country by the Hudson's Bay Company, but the local peoples resented the settlers' domineering ways. The Red River valley was populated by Assiniboine, Cree, and Métis, a people of mixed Cree and French blood. The traditional lifestyle of the Métis was a mix of

Plains Cree chief Mistahimaskwa (Big Bear) trades with Hudson's Bay Company agents at Fort Pitt on the North Saskatchewan River. (National Archives of Canada, PA 118768)

Indian and French culture. They made a living through trade, chiefly with North West Company agents in nearby Athabasca country.

Macdonnell immediately took measures to strengthen the Hudson's Bay Company's hold on Assiniboia. He prohibited the Métis to export pemmican, a nutrient-rich wilderness food, to North West Company agents in Athabasca country. The Métis ignored this restriction on a vital source of income, as well as the ban on running buffalo on horseback. Taking advantage of the resulting strain between Selkirk's settlers and the Métis, the North West Company armed the Métis and encouraged them to attack the whites. In 1815 the Métis raided Fort Douglas, forcing Macdonnell to surrender. The governor was arrested and sent to Montreal to face charges of incompetence, while Robert Semple was appointed to replace him.

The change of personnel did little to alleviate the troubles in Assiniboia. In 1816 a group of 60 Métis ambushed several Hudson's Bay Company supply boats and marched on Fort Douglas. Semple led 26 militiamen out to face the Métis, but he and more than 20 of his troops were killed in the skirmish. Taking matters into his own hands, Selkirk captured the North West Company's Fort William and moved against

THE EUROPEAN CONQUEST OF NORTH AMERICA

the Métis along the Red River. The Selkirk Treaty of 1817 ended the fighting for the time being, but in 1818 Selkirk was arrested in Upper Canada for his unauthorized activities and deported to England.

The competition between the Hudson's Bay and North West companies ended in 1821, when the two concerns merged under the name of the Hudson's Bay Company. Fort Garry replaced Fort Douglas as the company's headquarters in Assiniboia, but conflicts between whites and Métis continued. By 1836 most white colonists abandoned the area, and Assiniboia came under direct company management. The Hudson's Bay Company now controlled much of British North America, from Labrador to Oregon up to Alaska and the Arctic. The company's Fort Langley on the coast of Oregon was a major Pacific seaport, and steamships sailed regularly to Fort Vancouver in present-day Washington State. As the fur trade petered out, Hudson's Bay Company trading posts throughout the western part of British North America matured into agricultural and logging settlements.

PEOPLING THE PROVINCES

In 1815 Britain signed a treaty with the United States that formally concluded the War of 1812. (See Chapter 8.) Among other provisions, the treaty designated the 49th parallel as the border between the United States and British North America west of the Great Lakes. Within 30 years more than 730,000 British immigrants sailed to the colonies, half of them from famine-ravaged Ireland. Most immigrants arrived with nothing and faced an unknown future in the wilderness. Still, the majority never regretted their move. One immigrant wrote that

> [in Scotland] I had to labour sixteen or eighteen hours-a-day, and could earn about six or seven shillings-a-week—here, I can, by labouring about half that time, earn more than I need: there, I was confined to a damp shop,—but here, I enjoy fresh air . . . there, it is all dependence,—here, it is a fair prospect of independence.

From 1815 to 1830 the British authorities recruited settlers who received land grants when they arrived in the colonies. Both before and after the government program ended, other immigrants could purchase land from private entrepreneurs, who sometimes paid for their transportation from Britain. Ship owners and their agents advertised the charms of the colonies to immigrants who could pay for their passage. And some immigrants made their own arrangements, arriving independently to find their fortune on the frontier.

In the push west, the new arrivals were joined by settlers moving out of overpopulated eastern areas in search of better opportunities. Those with money became farmers, entrepreneurs, or artisans, while those without worked as laborers. The influx of settlers fueled the growth of the timber and grain industries, swelling demand for farmland and forest. More and more Indians were forced from their homes into less desirable or more remote territory; many died in plagues.

As the white population of British North America multiplied, the colonists of Upper and Lower Canada demanded a greater voice in government. Authority over every aspect of colonial life rested with the appointed governor and members of the colonial councils, while the elected assembly remained weak. During the 1820s critics of the colonial governor had gained a majority in the assembly of Upper Canada. Foremost among them was William Lyon Mackenzie, who published several critiques of the colonial government. The situation was similar in Lower Canada, where Louis-Joseph Papineau led the radicals. Outbursts of mob violence soon characterized elections in the two colonies.

The unrest erupted in the Rebellions of 1837. In Upper Canada, Mackenzie sought to transfer control of the government from the appointed elite to the elected assembly. In retaliation, the council dissolved the assembly and held a new election in which most of the reformers lost their seats. The rebellion in Lower Canada formed along racial lines, with French and English reformers each seeking to establish their own governments. Britain refused to extend home rule to the colonists, especially those with French blood.

In both Upper and Lower Canada, the political rebellion was accompanied by agrarian unrest. As the price of wheat plummeted on the world market, strapped farmers held protest meetings and engaged in several armed confrontations with colonial authorities. Papineau and

Mackenzie continued to seek a solution through political means, but they could not deal with an armed uprising. As the violence between rebels and government supporters intensified, both reformers fled to the United States. In the rebellion, a number of colonists were killed and some were arrested. The rebellion was put down within the year.

Fighting flared again, however, in the Lower Canadian Rebellion of 1838. Colonists who battled the British were routed, and many settlers' houses were burned. British soldiers captured 753 rebels, 12 of whom were executed and 58 of whom were sent to the British penal colony in Australia. In the aftermath of the rebellions, Parliament sent John George Lambton, the earl of Durham, to study the problems in the colonies. In 1839 he recommended that control of internal colonial affairs be turned over to the colonists to prevent further violence.

Lord Durham also suggested that the recalcitrant French be forced into submission by uniting Lower Canada with the much more populous and heavily English Upper Canada. He wrote:

> I entertain no doubts as to the national character which must be given to Lower Canada; it must be that of the British Empire, that of the majority of the population of British North America, that of the great race which must, in the lapse of no long period of time, be predominant over the whole North American continent. . . . There can hardly be conceived a nationality more destitute of all that can invigorate and elevate a people, than that which is exhibited by the descendants of the French in Lower Canada, owing to their retaining their peculiar language and manners. They are a people with no history and no literature.

Parliament implemented the second of Durham's recommendations in 1840, combining Upper and Lower Canada into the single Province of Canada. Quebec was now called Canada East and Ontario was called Canada West. Combined with the political maneuvering, the continued immigration of British subjects greatly weakened the position of the French in British North America. By 1845 the total white population of Britain's holdings was 1.6 million, including 600,000 people of French ancestry and 1 million people of British ancestry.

In addition, 150,000 Indians still lived in the unsettled territories to the west. The few Indians who remained in the settled areas were dying rapidly of European diseases. Robbed of their hunting grounds, they lived in poverty and depended on aid from the British government. By contrast, the white settlers prospered and continued to press west. As their population expanded, the settlers of British North America came into conflict with the equally mobile and even more numerous pioneers of the United States. Britain and the United States signed two treaties resolving their border disputes: the Webster-Ashburton Treaty of 1842, which set the border between Maine and New Brunswick, and the Oregon Boundary Treaty of 1846, which extended the western boundary between the two powers along the 49th parallel to the Pacific Ocean (excluding Vancouver Island, which became a British crown colony in 1848).

TOWARD CONFEDERATION

In 1848 Parliament acted on Durham's first recommendation, extending internal self-rule to the North American territories. In the west, meanwhile, the Hudson's Bay Company continued to grapple with the Métis in Rupert's Land. When the company tried to restrict Métis trade with the United States, the Métis turned to smuggling. In 1849 a Métis named Guillaume Sawyer was tried for smuggling, sparking the Courthouse Rebellion. Métis leader Louis Riel led 300 rebels to the Hudson's Bay Company post at Fort Garry to protest Sawyer's arrest. Although found guilty, Sawyer was set free and the Métis retained the right to free trade for the next 20 years.

Confrontations like the Courthouse Rebellion did not keep white settlers from the wide-open spaces of Rupert's Land. As settlers migrated away from the overpopulated east, they eyed the land held by the Hudson's Bay Company. The discovery of gold along the Thompson and Fraser rivers in British Columbia set off the gold rush of 1858, and the tiny village of Victoria became a boomtown. As whites flooded into the area and pushed the boundaries of mineral exploitation to the north, British Columbia was designated a crown colony. In the process, yet more Indians were forced off their land: Vancouver Island and British Columbia merged into the Province of British Columbia in 1866.

Britain seemed increasingly unwilling to spend much time, energy, or money on the provinces, even when the American Civil War gave the United States the military capability to annex British North America by force. Reluctant to finance the region's defense, Parliament urged the settlers to protect themselves. Throughout British North America, worries over the expanding United States mounted, and the need for a transcontinental railroad to facilitate settlement became obvious. The rival political parties in the Province of Canada responded to the situation by forming a coalition in 1864. The notion of gaining strength through unity filtered through the other provinces as well.

As settlers throughout the provinces developed a sense of their Canadian identity, they realized that westward expansion could be achieved best through organized cooperation among the provinces. Representatives of the maritime provinces—Nova Scotia, New Brunswick, Newfoundland, and Prince Edward Island—met at Charlottetown on Prince Edward Island in 1864 to discuss the possibility of unification. Later that year representatives of all the provinces assembled at the Quebec Conference.

After deciding that the benefits of unification outweighed the drawbacks, provincial representatives traveled to London to submit the Quebec Resolutions to Parliament. In 1867 the British North American Act was passed, confederating the provinces of Canada, Nova Scotia, and New Brunswick into the Dominion of Canada and splitting the Province of Canada into Ontario and Quebec. British Columbia would join the confederation in 1871 and Prince Edward Island in 1873.

In 1869 the First Dominion Parliament purchased Rupert's Land from the Hudson's Bay Company and renamed it the Northwest Territories. As white settlers flowed into the territories, a smallpox epidemic killed more than 2,000 Indians, and conflicts with the Métis arose. Many of the settlers were fervent Protestants who hated French Catholics. These settlers were also annexationists who hated the Indians standing in the way of white expansion. The Métis, who represented all things French and Indian, received only the settlers' scorn. The white disregard for Métis rights soon led to the First Riel Rebellion.

When government surveyors arrived to lay out 800-acre townships that encroached on Métis territory, the Métis protested. Led by Louis Riel (son of the Courthouse Rebellion leader), 16 Métis chased the surveyors off their land. Riel then organized the Comité National de

Métis and took 400 Métis to block the approach of William McDougall, the territorial governor. After forcing MacDougall to retreat, Riel traveled to the capital in Ottawa with a List of Rights, which demanded secure land, a voice in government, and free religion for the Métis. Parliament stalled while MacDougall led a small militia into the contested territory and demanded that the Métis surrender.

Settlers also organized to fight the Métis, but the Métis had greater numbers and superior firepower. In a fight at Fort Garry, the whites were defeated and taken prisoner. MacDougall was expelled once again, and the Métis Comité set up a provisional government with Riel as president. Riel released the white prisoners, but when he got wind of their plans for another fight, he arrested them again and sentenced one to death. The execution angered Parliament, which passed the 1870 Manitoba Act carving a new province from the Northwest Territories around the Red River. A large force of white policemen was sent to Manitoba and harassed Riel until he fled to Montana. The white settlers' continued abuse eventually prompted most Métis to move west to the Saskatchewan River.

To keep the peace on the frontier, the Dominion Parliament organized the North West Mounted Police (the Mounties) in 1873. The Mounties set up six posts among the Indians by 1875 and during the 1870s negotiated seven treaties in which the Indians gave up large amounts of land. In 1876 the Canadian Indian Act further defined Indian policy, extending the vote to Indians who gave up their Indian rights to become Canadian citizens. But by the end of that decade the buffalo was almost extinct in Canada, and famine hit the Indians hard. Construction of the Canadian Pacific Railroad from Montreal to Vancouver from 1881 to 1885 brought a flood of whites to the west. The Canadian government tried to absorb Indians into Canadian society, but most Indians resisted.

White settlement advanced inexorably, reaching the Saskatchewan River in 1884. As they had along the Red River, government surveyors started breaking up Métis lands. When their protests were ignored, the Métis brought Louis Riel back to Canada to help. Riel's attempts at peaceful negotiation failed, and the Second Riel Rebellion began. The Métis sabotaged white settlements and took white hostages, then demanded that the Mounties leave Fort Carlton. In 1885 a force of 55

Mounties and 55 volunteers tried to capture the Métis trading post at Duck Lake, but after 10 Mounties were killed and 14 wounded, the whites retreated.

Mounty reinforcements arrived at Fort Carlton while Riel enlisted the support of two Cree chiefs, Poundmaker and Wandering Spirit. After the Cree attacked two white settlements, the Dominion Parliament established the North West Field Force to crush the insurrection. Eight thousand troops arrived in the region on the newly completed Canadian Pacific Railroad, where they coped with repeated Métis and Cree ambushes. The Indians held out until 900 government reinforcements arrived. The revitalized white army defeated the Métis at Batoche, and the Cree surrendered. When Riel was executed for treason, Indian resistance to white settlement was virtually extinguished throughout Canada.

The white conquest of Canada concluded with the Klondike Gold Rush of 1896 to 1898, which established a white population in northern Canada. Alberta and Saskatchewan became Canadian provinces in 1905, while the Ungava Peninsula was attached to Quebec. The last provinces to join the confederation were Manitoba,

The 1885 trial of Métis leader Louis Riel for treason. (National Archives of Canada, C-1879)

in 1912, and Newfoundland, in 1949. Far to the north, Yukon Territory and the remainder of the Northwest Territories have yet to achieve provincial status.

CHAPTER SEVEN NOTES

p. 95   "... highly Advantageous in ..." Quoted in Bumsted. p. 176.

p. 95   "... a total exclusion of ..." Quoted in Bumsted. p176.

p. 99   "... [in Scotland] I had to ..." Quoted in Bumsted. p. 187.

p. 101   "I entertain no ..." Quoted in J. Bartlet Brebner. pp. 222–23.

MANIFEST DESTINY IN THE UNITED STATES

In 1790 the 13 United States of America—Connecticut, Delaware, Georgia, Maryland, Massachusetts, New Hampshire, New Jersey, New York, North Carolina, Pennsylvania, Rhode Island, South Carolina, and Virginia—stretched out along the Atlantic coast of North America and extended a few miles inland. The new nation had a Constitution, a president (George Washington), a Congress, and a capital in Philadelphia. Plans were under way for a permanent capital on the Potomac River; the federal government would move to Washington, D.C. in 1800. The first national census, taken in 1790, placed the population of the country at almost 4 million, a figure that included about 700,000 slaves. The United States held title to almost all of North America east of the Mississippi River and south of the Great Lakes, except for Spanish Florida (which included the southern parts of present-day Mississippi and Alabama) and the northern hump of Maine, which was claimed by both the United States and Britain.

Congress formed three new states before the end of the 18th century: Vermont in 1791, Kentucky in 1792, and Tennessee in 1796.

Americans already thought of the whole of North America as their own. In 1819 Secretary of State John Quincy Adams reflected the attitude of many when he stated that the prospect of a United States takeover of all North America was "as much a law of nature . . . as that the Mississippi should flow into the sea." In the 1840s the idea became known as "Manifest Destiny." Throughout the 19th century Americans pursued this vision, moving west along with large numbers of European immigrants. More than 5 million immigrants arrived on American shores and spread out across the continent before the Civil War; after the war millions more came. The immigrants helped conquer the continent.

As white settlers pushed west, they encountered both Indians who had previously been forced out of the east and indigenous peoples. During the first half of the 19th century, the War Department controlled official relations with the Indians. Initial attempts to protect Indians or absorb them into white society included the 1802 ban on the sale of liquor to Indians and congressional allotment of funds for their "civilization" and education. But it was apparent that restless white settlers and independent Indians could not live together peacefully. In 1825 Congress set aside Indian Country, a tract of land west of the Mississippi River between the Red and Missouri rivers, and started forcing eastern Indians to move there.

Congress chose this territory because it did not think that whites would settle between the Mississippi and the Rockies. The plains and prairies, which lacked water and timber, were called the Great American Desert. Early settlers considered the region an obstacle to be passed on the way to the mineral-rich mountains or the fertile Pacific coast. Officially defined Indian lands on the Great Plains came to be called Indian Territory, a zone that shrank steadily and ultimately became the State of Oklahoma.

Most white settlers of the American West held a low opinion of the "savages" who stood in the way of their aspirations. They angered Indians by ignoring the boundaries set up by treaties, by killing off game, and by turning hunting grounds into farms. Violence was inevitable, and soon government policy formalized the pattern of forcible

Indian eviction. The army built dozens of forts to serve as bases for the protection of white settlers, while American law made Indians foreigners in their own land. Government agents tricked or bullied the Indians into signing treaties that took their land and offered no lasting security. In the 19th century the United States conducted a series of major military campaigns against the Indians to free up land for white use. The few Indians who survived the onslaught were relegated to tiny reservations, and the European conquest of North America was complete.

THE OLD NORTHWEST AND THE MIDWEST

When the United States gained its independence, many indigenous (Miami, Potawatomi, Sauk, Fox, Shawnee, etc.) and displaced (Ottawa, Ojibwa, Algonkin, Delaware, Iroquois, etc.) tribes lived in the Northwest Territory. The Indians soon encountered white settlers who moved in to claim farmland. Miami chief Little Turtle organized a confederacy of Miami, Shawnee, Ojibwa, Delaware, Potawatomi, and Ottawa to stage a rebellion. Military and diplomatic efforts to pacify the Indians failed until General Anthony Wayne led 3,000 U.S. troops to the region in 1794. Little Turtle advised his people to make peace before any more blood was shed, but the angry Indians wanted to fight and chose Turkey Foot as their new leader.

The rebellion came to an end at Fallen Timbers on the western shore of Lake Erie. In a surprise attack, the Americans burned a number of Indian villages and killed many Indians. Defeated, the Indians were forced to sign the 1795 Treaty of Fort Greenville, in which they ceded much of present-day Ohio and Indiana to the United States, along with other strategic points in the Northwest Territory. Ohio achieved statehood in 1803.

The United States also used subtler methods to gain land from the Indians. Until 1822 the War Department operated trading "factories" in Indian country, where government agents encouraged Indians to accumulate debt. When a tribe's bill grew large enough, the agents would persuade them to pay it off by ceding land. In theory, the Indians would then be moved to agricultural reservations and would learn to live like whites. Faced with the loss of their land, Northwest Territory Indians sought strength in religion, tradition, and political union. In

1799 Handsome Lake, half brother of Seneca chief Cornplanter, founded the Longhouse religion, while in the early 1800s the Shawnee visionary Tenskwatawa, known as the Prophet, preached the rejection of white ways. The Prophet's brother, Shawnee chief Tecumseh, advocated intertribal unity and Indian resistance to the whites. Traveling from the Great Lakes to the Gulf of Mexico, Tecumseh tried to convince various tribes to treat all unceded Indian land as commonly held and thus unsellable. The Ojibwa, Winnebago, and Potawatomi agreed to Tecumseh's plan, but other bands ignored his warnings and continued to sell land to white settlers.

In 1811, when Tecumseh and his federation refused to recognize these sales, Indiana governor William Henry Harrison marched on their settlement at Tippecanoe. Tecumseh was away on one of his diplomatic missions, and his brother ambushed the white troops. Harrison overwhelmed the Indians, burning the town. The defeat shattered the union Tecumseh had struggled to build.

By then the white population of the United States had topped 7 million, and about 1 million settlers lived west of the Allegheny Mountains. Across the Mississippi River, Missouri was organized as a territory in 1812. As sporadic Indian raids continued along the border with British North America, the United States began to suspect they were encouraged by the English. That border was still in dispute, as were shipping rights along the Atlantic coast and in the Great Lakes. The American Revolution had produced bad feelings on both sides, and many Americans wanted to push the British out of North America for good and annex Canada.

The War of 1812, sometimes called the Second American Revolution, started when the United States declared war on Britain. Embittered by his recent defeat, Tecumseh joined with the British and led the Indian fight to retake land from the Americans. Tecumseh was killed in battle and the war reached a stalemate. In 1814 the opponents signed the Treaty of Ghent, allowing Americans to move into previously disputed territory south of the 49th parallel.

As the white population of the Old Northwest grew, Indiana became a state in 1816 and Illinois in 1818. Congress attempted to resolve the dispute over whether slavery should be allowed to expand to the west by passing the Missouri Compromise in 1820.

The measure admitted Missouri to the union as a slave state, admitted Maine (previously a part of Massachusetts) as a free state, organized Arkansas as a slave territory, and prohibited slavery in future territories and states north of 36°30′ in the Louisiana Purchase (excluding Missouri).

Over the next 40 years, thousands of white settlers abandoned the overcrowded East for the rich farmland of the Midwest. Wheat farming boomed from Michigan and Indiana in the east to Nebraska and Kansas in the west and from Missouri in the south to Minnesota and Wisconsin in the north. After the factory system was abolished in 1822, the United States continued to sign and break treaties with the Indians, forcing most Northwest Territory tribes to move west of the Mississippi. The Indians did not go without a fight, however. The Winnebago Uprising (1826–27)flared in northwest Illinois and southwest Wisconsin, and the Kickapoo Resistance (1819–32) erupted in Illinois.

The Black Hawk War broke out when Sauk chief Black Hawk rejected a fraudulent 1804 treaty in which Harrison had tricked some Sauk and Fox chiefs out of their land by getting them drunk. Refusing to vacate his village at Rock Island, Illinois, he was joined by Fox, Winnebago, Potawatomi, and Kickapoo Indians. When white troops marched to the Rock River in 1832, Black Hawk sent a truce party

U.S. Army officers smoke tobacco with Indian leaders, signifying their intent to maintain peaceful relations. (Picture Collection, The Branch Libraries, The New York Public Library)

to negotiate, but the soldiers killed three of the party and the Indians attacked. The Americans pursued the Indians to the junction of the Mississippi and Bad Axe rivers in Wisconsin and massacred them while they were trying to flee across the Mississippi to Indian Territory.

Whites also fought among themselves in such conflicts as the border dispute between Ohio and Michigan from 1835 to 1837, known as the Toledo War. In 1842 the Webster-Ashburton Treaty resolved some American-British border disputes, setting the northern borders of Maine and Minnesota. By then the population of the United States exceeded 17 million people, about 6 million of whom lived west of the Alleghenies. Before 1860 Michigan, Iowa, Wisconsin, and Minnesota gained statehood.

THE SOUTHEAST

The United States faced the first challenge to its southeastern claims in the 1790s, not from Indians but from other Europeans. At that time Spain, which held title to Louisiana, broke with its ally Britain and sought the support of the United States in the New World. The new allies signed Pinckney's Treaty in 1795, in which Spain gave up its claim to the southern parts of present-day Alabama and Mississippi, agreed to set the northern border of Florida at the 31st parallel, and opened the Mississippi River to American shipping. Congress then organized the territories of Alabama and Mississippi and set the boundaries of Georgia.

Spain broke the treaty in 1800, when it made a secret agreement with Napoleon that returned Louisiana to France. When France closed the mouth of the Mississippi to American ships, the United States offered to buy the territory for $15 million, and the Louisiana Purchase was concluded in 1803. The last French governor of Louisiana marveled at the rate of American expansion into the south, writing

> They set up their huts, cut and burn the timber, kill the savages or are killed by them, and disappear from the country either by dying or ceding to some steadfast cultivator the land they have already begun to clear. When a score of new colonists are thus gathered in a certain spot . . . they beget children without end;

they vainly advertise vast territories for sale; they attract and deceive as many buyers as possible; they increase the figures of the population till they reach a total of 60,000 souls, at which time they are able to form an independent state and send a representative to Congress . . . and there is one more star in the United States flag.

Louisiana became a state in 1812. Farther north, American settlers had problems with the Upper Creek Indians (known as the Red Sticks), who were inspired by Tecumseh to stand fast against white encroachment. In 1814 Andrew Jackson allied with the pro-white Lower Creek Indians (White Sticks) and Cherokee and moved against the Red Sticks. A series of skirmishes culminated in the Battle of Horseshoe Bend, where 750 of 900 Red Sticks were killed. With the Red Stick surrender, the Creek ceded 23 million acres (much of Georgia and Alabama) to the United States. Three years later, in 1817, Mississippi became a state; in 1819 Alabama followed suit.

Spain also angered the United States by allowing the Seminole of Florida to harbor runaway slaves. In 1818 Jackson commanded American troops in the First Seminole War, capturing the Spanish fort at Pensacola and claiming West Florida for the United States. Spain ceded Florida in 1819, and in 1822 the region was organized as a territory. White settlers began to arrive, pushing the Seminole onto a small reservation.

Land-hungry whites in Alabama, Mississippi, and especially Georgia terrorized and massacred Indians, forcing the federal government to step in. In 1830, backed by recently elected President Andrew Jackson, Congress passed the Indian Removal Act. The law gave the president the authority to offer the "Five Civilized Tribes" (the Cherokee, Choctaw, Creek, Chickasaw, and Seminole) land in the Indian Territory in exchange for land in the southern states. The Five Civilized Tribes got their name because many of them had adapted to white ways.

The Indians' "civilized" ways, however, did not impress settlers who wanted more land. Jackson justified Indian removal as a way to protect Indians, stating that it will separate the Indians from immediate contact with settlements of whites; free them from the power of the States; enable them to pursue happiness in their own way and under their own rude institutions; will retard the progress of decay, which is lessening their numbers, and perhaps cause them gradually, under the protection of the Government and through the influence of good counsels, to cast off their savage habits and become an interesting, civilized and Christian community.

However it was rationalized, the removal of tens of thousands of Indians from the southern states and territories under Jackson and his successor, Martin Van Buren, freed up huge tracts of land for white settlement. American troops escorted the Choctaw to Indian Territory between 1831 and 1834, then the Creek in 1836 and the Chickasaw in 1837. Many Indians died on the long walk west because of insufficient supplies of food and other essentials as well as harsh weather, disease, and raids by bandits. Even more died after reaching their new land, which offered only the meagerest living. When the United States tried to force the Seminole out of Florida in 1835, the Indians struck back and the Second Seminole War began. Numerous indecisive battles killed large numbers of white troops while edging the Seminole back. At one point the army managed to send 3,000 Indians west, but others escaped and took refuge in the Everglades. In 1842 the United States finally abandoned the costly effort.

The Cherokee fought removal in a different way, taking their case all the way to the Supreme Court. In 1832 the Court decided in favor of the Indians, but President Jackson ignored the decision and sent the army to round them up. The soldiers marched them west on a miserable trek that came to be called the Trail of Tears. Pummeled by harsh weather, starvation, disease, exposure, and bandit raids on the 800-mile trip, 4,000 of the Cherokee died before reaching Indian Territory. Several hundred, however, managed to escape capture and hid in the mountains of North Carolina, where today they are known as the Eastern Cherokee. Few other Indians remained in the Southeast. White success in the region made Arkansas a state in 1836 and Florida one in 1845. The last significant Indian resistance in the area was the Third Seminole Uprising of 1855 to 1858. In the aftermath of the conflict, more Seminole were sent to Indian Territory, although a few remained in the Everglades.

FROM THE MOUNTAINS TO THE SEA

While some American settlers pushed steadily west from the East Coast, others leapfrogged all the way to the Rocky Mountains and the West Coast. Americans first explored the Columbia River of the Pacific Northwest in 1792. Sent out to map the Louisiana Purchase, the 1804–6 expedition of Meriwether Lewis and William Clark charted the High Plains, the northern Rockies, the Columbia Plateau, and the Cascade Mountains. In its wake, the American fur trade advanced up the Missouri River to Blackfoot and Shoshoni country, where contact with white traders spread European diseases among the Indians. Indian life also was threatened by the arrival of British and American missionaries, who undermined Indian culture in their efforts to win new converts and bring more settlers to Oregon Country.

After John Charles Frémont and Kit Carson explored Oregon Country, many Americans turned their eyes to the Far West. The Russians, meanwhile, abandoned the area in 1841 when competition in the fur trade overwhelmed them. In 1840 the first American pioneers settled in the Willamette Valley, whose Indians had been wiped out by disease. As Oregon Fever set in, wagon trains poured into Oregon Country via the Oregon Trail. The 2,100-mile trip from Independence, Missouri took six months to complete, but Americans went to Oregon by the thousands. As the United States secured its claim to the Pacific Northwest, it signed a 1846 treaty with Britain that set the 49th parallel as the border between Oregon and British North America.

As it did everywhere, the white arrival in the Far West ignited violence. From 1847 to 1880 virtually every tribe from the mountains to the sea fought white expansion. In every case the Indians lost; some were sent to Indian Territory, some were relegated to small reservations closer to home, and others fled to more remote land. In 1859 Oregon became a state, but tensions in the region only worsened with the discovery of gold on a Nez Percé reservation in 1860. As white miners rushed in, the Indians were forced to sign a treaty requiring them to move to another, much smaller reservation. Some of the Nez Percé, including a band led by Chief Joseph (who never signed the

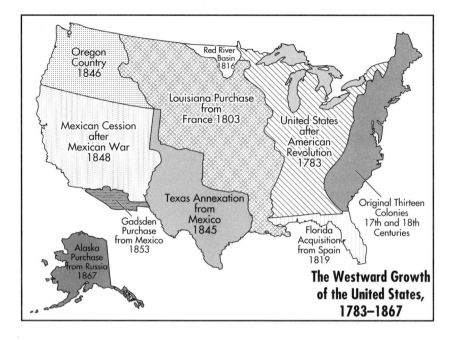

The Westward Growth of the United States, 1783–1867

treaty), refused to leave voluntarily. In 1877 United States troops arrived to enforce the treaty. Holding off the Americans, the Nez Percé fled to the east. The army pursued them all the way to northern Montana, where Chief Joseph surrendered after a five-day battle. Almost all the region's Indians were forced onto reservations by 1880. In 1889 Washington became a state, and in 1890 Idaho did as well.

Down the coast, the Mexican government (which had won its independence from Spain in 1821) closed the Catholic missions of California, impoverishing many "mission Indians" who had depended on them. California became a United States territory when Mexico ceded it in 1848, a year before the gold rush started. The discovery of gold in California brought 100,000 white settlers to the territory in 1849, and that number kept growing. Whites overran Indian lands and massacred many Indians or forced them into slavery or prostitution. Fighting between whites and Indians killed perhaps 70,000 indigenous Californians by 1859 and forced the rest onto reservations, where they died of starvation and disease. Meanwhile, the ongoing debate over slavery in the United States produced the Compromise of 1850, in which California was admitted

Prospectors pan for gold in Dakota Territory. (Library of Congress)

to the union as a free state. The Modoc War of 1872–73, led by a man named Captain Jack or Kintpuash, was the last Indian resistance in California.

Brigham Young led the first of 15,000 Mormons to the Great Salt Lake and founded the independent republic of Deseret in 1847. Under the Compromise of 1850, Congress organized the region as Utah Territory. To the east, prospectors found gold at Pike's Peak in 1858, setting off the Colorado gold rush. In Nevada, discovery of the Comstock Lode started another gold rush the same year. The influx of whites kindled the 1860 Paiute War in Nevada, the 1863 Shoshoni War in Utah and Idaho, and the 1879 Ute War in Colorado. Indians were forced onto reservations and white settlers took over their land. Nevada achieved statehood in 1864, Colorado in 1876, and Utah in 1896.

TEXAS AND THE SOUTHWEST
Mexican independence from Spain opened the Southwest to American trade. During the 1820s and 1830s, Americans carried goods along the Santa Fe Trail and the Colorado River, selling them for gold and silver. In the process, they sometimes skirmished with Comanche, Yuma, and

ALASKA

Although Alaska did not witness the white-Indian warfare common to the more southerly parts of North America, its indigenous peoples were equally ravaged by the white invasion. During the 1790s Russia had a monopoly on the fur trade in Alaska, a name that corrupted the Aleut's term for "great land" or "that which the sea breaks against." The Russians were very cruel to the Aleutian people among whom they lived, and the Aleutian population declined rapidly as a result of Russian abuse and epidemics of diseases carried by the traders. After the Russian American Company obtained a royal charter from Czar Paul I in 1799, it employed many Aleuts in the fur trade.

Throughout the 19th century, however, the Tlingit people fiercely resisted the Russian presence in their land. Refusing to trade with the whites, they attacked the intruders with firearms purchased from British and American traders. The Tlingit killed many Russians and captured their posts, keeping a tenuous grasp on their land. More whites began to appear in Alaska in 1848 and started whaling off its shores. But the Russians grew frustrated with Indian interference and in 1867 sold Alaska to the United States. In 1884 Congress agreed to accept the Indians' title to Alaskan land. White settlers cared little for legal niceties and swarmed through Indian territory during the Klondike Gold Rush of 1896 to 1898. A permanent white presence was established, but Alaska did not become a state until 1959.

Mojave Indians. Americans from the Southeast filtered west at the same time, settling in Texas. Worried by the growing American presence, Mexico halted the migration in 1830. The Anglo settlers already in Texas also faced resentment from Comanche, Kiowa, and Apache Indians, with whom they fought frequently.

Mexico declined U.S. offers to purchase Texas, but Anglos there took matters into their own hands in 1836, when they declared the independence of the Lone Star Republic. Mexico sent General Antonio López de Santa Anna to put down the rebellion, and in a war that included the famous battle for the Alamo, the Texans under Sam Houston finally won. The newly independent Lone Star Republic petitioned Congress for statehood, which because of disputes over slavery was not granted until 1845. The entrance of Texas into the union angered Mexico, which had feared United States penetration of the region.

The Mexican War broke out the following year. American forces invaded Mexico, New Mexico, Arizona, and California, fighting not only the Mexicans but the Pueblo Indians. The United States won the war in 1848 and Mexico signed the Treaty of Guadelupe Hidalgo, ceding the Southwest and California north of the Gila River. The United States finalized its border with Mexico with the Gadsden Purchase of 1853, in which Mexico sold a strip of land south of the Gila River. (The area now makes up southern Arizona and New Mexico.)

Until 1886 Americans faced fierce Indian resistance in the southwest and Texas. United States troops ranged through the area battling Comanche, Kiowa, Kickapoo, Yuma, and Mojave Indians. Colonel Kit Carson commanded American forces in the Navajo War from 1863 to 1866 in New Mexico and Arizona, forcing the Navajo to make the 300-mile "Long Walk" to a reservation in 1864. Provoked by white abuses, Indians in Arizona launched the Apache Uprising in 1861. The 25-year war ended in 1886, when Geronimo, a chief who had eluded capture by hiding along the Mexican border, finally surrendered. His defeat ended Indian resistance in the Southwest; in 1912 New Mexico and Arizona became states.

THE FINAL CONQUEST

White expansion from the east, south, and west ultimately threatened the last free Indian land: the Great Plains. Starting in the 1840s, whites crossed the Mississippi River into territory occupied by displaced eastern Indian tribes, forcing them into Indian Territory. Cholera epidemics raged through the region in the 1850s, while pioneer wagon trains on their way to the West Coast interfered with Indian buffalo hunting, the core of Plains culture. In 1851 the United States signed a treaty with the Plains Indians guaranteeing the security of their hunting grounds in return for the safe passage of wagon trains. Troops were stationed at Fort Laramie, Wyoming to monitor adherence to the treaty. The Kansas-Nebraska Act of 1854 carved a big chunk out of Indian Territory to create Kansas and Nebraska territories.

A three-year rebellion of Sioux on the northern plains was followed by resistance among the Cheyenne of Kansas and Nebraska. The army put down both uprisings, and in 1861 Kansas was admitted to the union as a free state. White settlers streamed west after the passage of the 1862 Homestead Act, which opened large tracts of Indian land in Kansas and Nebraska. By living on the land for five years, a settler could earn the deed to a 160-acre plot. To free the plains of Indians, the federal government encouraged the mass slaughter of buffalo. The Indians fought back. Across the plains, Cheyenne, Sioux, and Arapaho Indians battled white advancement throughout the Civil War. Most U.S. troops had been diverted to fight the war in the East, but the white settlers raised militias that managed to hold the Indians at bay.

When the Civil War ended in 1865, a new wave of settlers— veterans, former slaves, displaced Southerners, and others—swept onto the plains. Nebraska became a state in 1867, and Texas ranchers started driving their cattle north to Missouri and Kansas for shipment east by rail. The Transcontinental Railroad linking the East and West coasts was completed in 1869, when the Union Pacific and Central Pacific companies joined their tracks at Promontory Point, Utah. By the 1880s the cattle boom transformed the plains. Huge herds of longhorns trampled buffalo country, and wild cowtowns, such as Abilene, Ellsworth, Wichita, and Dodge City, Kansas, sprouted. Army troops arrived in the region to deal with the Indians, and the savage last chapter of the North American conquest began.

Tribes in Indian Territory were forced onto smaller and smaller plots as other tribes were driven into the area. Both in Indian Territory and elsewhere, the reservations were located on poor land where it was difficult to make a living. Each time it established a reservation, the United States believed it had found a permanent solution to the Indian "problem." In 1867 one Indian commisioner remarked, "That these reservations will cause any considerable annoyance to whites we do not believe. They consist, for the most part, of ground unfitted for cultivation, but suited to the peculiar habits of the Indians." But settlers continued to demand more land, and the reservations shrank rapidly.

Of course, the Plains Indians defied efforts to confine them to reservations and tried to block further buffalo slaughters and settlement by whites. Determined to secure the entire United States for its white citizens, in 1871 the federal government abandoned its policy of recognizing Indian tribes as sovereign nations and signing treaties with them. Indians were barred from leaving the reservations without permission. Wars involving the Sioux, Cheyenne, Arapaho, Kiowa, and Comanche raged across the plains in the 1860s and 1870s.

In 1874 gold was discovered on the Cheyenne reservation in the Black Hills of South Dakota, Montana, and Wyoming. White miners rushed to the area, but the Indians refused to sell the United States that part of their reservation, which was sacred. Ordered to vacate the Black Hills, many of the Cheyenne balked. In the Sioux War of 1876–77, Sioux chiefs Sitting Bull and Crazy Horse came to the assistance of the Cheyenne. The most famous encounter of that war was the Battle of Little Bighorn. On June 25, 1877 Colonel George A. Custer attacked the camp of Crazy Horse and Sitting Bull, which was located on the Little Bighorn River. The Indians won a stunning victory, killing Custer and 225 of his soldiers. But they lost the war, with some escaping to Canada while others were sent to reservations.

White hunters wiped out the last great buffalo herd in 1885. New railroads inched their way through the Great Plains in the 1880s, making much of the region easily accessible to settlers. Before long, whites who called themselves Boomers were squatting on 150 million acres of reservation land in Indian Territory. Congress responded to pressure from the Boomers in 1887, passing the General Allotment (Dawes Severalty) Act. The act broke many of the Indian Territory reservations into smaller tracts that were allotted to individual Indians. After 25 years of living on their lots, the Indians could gain full possession of the land. Or they could sell their rights to the government and move to a nonallotted reservation. Under the act, the federal government bought 2 million acres of land in Indian Territory and transferred it to settlers in the Oklahoma Land Run of 1889. Settlers gathered at a designated starting point, and when the signal was given,

Plains Indian warriors call on their equestrian skills in battle against white settlers.
(Library of Congress)

they literally raced to claim homesteads. In 1890 Oklahoma Territory was organized; it became a state in 1907.

In 1889 North Dakota, South Dakota, and Montana entered the union, followed by Wyoming in 1890. As their culture crumbled, the Plains Indians sought power in the Ghost Dance religion led by a Paiute prophet named Wovoka. The religion, which prophesied an end to white power, spread rapidly among the Indians. In its campaign to eradicate the movement, the United States dealt the final blow to the Plains Indians. The army marched through the plains in search of Ghost Dance adherents. In 1890 white soldiers killed Sitting Bull while trying to arrest him, then massacred 150 Sioux Indians at Wounded Knee, South Dakota. These two events crushed the Ghost Dance religion and completed the European conquest of North America.

Black Elk, an Oglala Sioux holy man, witnessed the massacre at Wounded Knee. In his old age he reflected on the event's significance:

THE EUROPEAN CONQUEST OF NORTH AMERICA

I did not know then how much was ended. When I look back . . . I can still see the butchered women and children lying heaped and scattered all along the crooked gulch. . . . And I can see that something else died there in the bloody mud, and was buried in the blizzard. A people's dream died there. . . . The nation's hoop is broken and scattered. There is no center any longer, and the sacred tree is dead.

By the time of the Wounded Knee massacre, fewer than 250,000 Indians lived on only 60 million acres in the United States. According to the 1890 census, at least two people per square mile lived everywhere in the nation: There was no more frontier. In an 1893 paper titled "The Significance of the Frontier in American History," Frederick Jackson Turner wrote of the white conquest of the continent. "Four centuries from the discovery of America," he reflected, "at the end of a hundred years under the Constitution, the frontier has gone and with its going has closed the first period of American history."

CHAPTER EIGHT NOTES

p. 108   ". . . as much a law of . . ." Quoted in Winthrop D. Jordan, et al. *The United States: Conquering a Continent* (Englewood Cliffs, NJ: Prentice-Hall, 1987), 6th ed., vol. 1, p. 185.

pp. 112–113   "They set up their . . ." Quoted in Jordan, et al. p. 198.

p. 114   ". . . will separate the . . ." Quoted in Jordan, et al. p. 223.

pp. 120–121   "That these reservations . . ." Quoted in Tindall. p. 766.

p. 123   "I did not know . . ." Quoted in Jordan, et al. p. 410.

p. 123   "Four centuries from the . . ." Quoted in Tindall. p. 774.

THE PLACE OF THE CONQUEST IN WORLD HISTORY

The European conquest of North America repre-
sents one of the most important periods in recorded history. On every
level of human endeavor, it heralded the dawn of a new age. The New
World served as a stage upon which European rivalries were played
out, resulting in a shift in the balance of European power that would
determine the direction of future world history. North America also
played an important part in the expansion of the world's economy.
Europe gained enormous wealth by its conquest and found both a
source of raw materials for its growing industries and a market for the
products produced by those industries. And after North American
whites took control of their own destiny, they built robust economies
that gave birth to entirely new industries.

The success of European colonialism in the New World spurred European conquest in Asia and Africa. African civilizations were annihilated by the white hunger for slaves to work the plantations of North America. Exploration fever sent European adventurers not only over the Atlantic Ocean and across the unknown continent but into Africa and around the South Seas. In the process, the peoples of the world learned a great deal about each other.

From the Native Americans, Europeans learned about canoes, snowshoes, moccasins, dogsleds, and other useful items. Sea otter and buffalo hides had never been seen in Europe before. The Old World also gained maize (corn), potatoes, peanuts, turkey, squash, tomatoes, peppers, many types of beans, and other new foods from North America. And the Indians taught the Europeans how to smoke tobacco and may have infected them with syphilis. In the other direction, whites introduced firearms, metal blades, glass, and other inventions to North America. They imported horses, pigs, cattle, goats, sheep, and maybe chickens as well as melons, wheat, rice, oats, and other crops. Along with alcohol, which killed many Indians who had no notion of its power, Europeans brought diseases such as smallpox, measles, and typhus to the continent.

Of course, the European conquest of North America all but extinguished the continent's indigenous cultures. Untold numbers of Native Americans died of European diseases or were killed by white invaders. Those who survived lost their ancestral homelands and were forced onto reservations where they have since endured profound poverty and neglect. The white conquerors, meanwhile, created two new nations— the United States and Canada—with unique characters all their own. In the course of their conquest of the continent, white North Americans learned lessons of independence, brashness, self-sufficiency, optimism, and versatility. Far more populous than its northern neighbor, the United States used those lessons to become the single most powerful nation on earth.

CHRONOLOGY

33,000 B.C. •	Humans start migrating to North America over the land bridge across the Bering Strait.
100 B.C.– • A.D. 700	The peoples of the Hopewell Culture build large burial mounds in the Ohio, Mississippi, and Illinois river valleys.
986 •	Biarni Heriulfson, a Norse Viking, sails to Baffin Island.
1000 •	Viking Leif Eriksson reaches Newfoundland, which he calls Vinland.
1003 •	The Vikings establish a fishing colony on Vinland. They leave in 1015.
1492–93 •	Christopher Columbus makes his first voyage to the New World, sighting land in the Caribbean on October 12, 1492.
1497–98 •	John Cabot explores Newfoundland for England.
1500s •	The Mississippian Culture (founded in the eighth century) reaches its peak in the Southeast.
1501 •	Gaspar Corte-Real explores Labrador and Newfoundland for Portugal.
1513 •	Juan Ponce de León lands on the Florida peninsula and claims it for Spain.

1523–24	•	Florentine navigator Giovanni da Verrazano explores the coast from Carolina to Newfoundland for France.
1528–36	•	Spanish adventurers Álvar Núñez Cabeza de Vaca and Estevanico wander from the Gulf of Mexico to the Southwest.
1534–42	•	Jacques Cartier makes three voyages to the St. Lawrence River for France.
1539–43	•	Hernando de Soto explores the Southeast for Spain.
1540–42	•	Francisco Vásquez de Coronado treks from Mexico to Kansas in search of gold for Spain.
1560s	•	The Mohawk, Oneida, Onondaga, Cayuga, and Seneca peoples form the League of Five Nations.
	•	France attempts to found two settlements in Florida but fails.
1565	•	Spain establishes St. Augustine, Florida.
1576–78	•	Martin Frobisher explores Arctic Canada for England.
1578–79	•	Sir Francis Drake sails to California and claims it for England.
1583	•	Sir Humphrey Gilbert makes an aborted attempt to colonize Newfoundland for England.
1584–90	•	Sir Walter Raleigh makes two attempts to establish an English settlement on Roanoke Island. Both fail.
1598	•	Juan de Oñate founds a Spanish settlement in Pueblo Indian country. Fighting between Spanish and Indians lasts until 1599.
1603–15	•	Samuel de Champlain explores from Nova Scotia to the Great Lakes for France. He founds Port Royal (present-day Annapolis Royal) on Nova Scotia in 1605 and Quebec City in 1608.
1607	•	English settlers found Jamestown, Virginia.
1609	•	Sailing for the Dutch East India Company, Henry Hudson finds New York Harbor and the Hudson River.

1610	•	The Spanish found Santa Fe as the capital of New Mexico.
	•	Henry Hudson explores Hudson Bay and James Bay.
1614	•	The first shipment of tobacco reaches England from Virginia.
1620	•	The English Pilgrims found Plymouth Colony.
1621	•	King James VI of Scotland (James I of England) grants Nova Scotia to Sir William Alexander.
1622	•	Powhatan Indians kill 347 of Virginia's 1,200 white inhabitants. War ensues.
1624	•	The Dutch build Fort Orange as a base for trade with the Iroquois.
1626	•	The Dutch buy Manhattan Island for goods worth 60 guilders ($24.00). The colony of New Amsterdam forms.
1627–32	•	War between France and England. England acquires New France, but returns it in 1632 under the treaty of Saint-Germain-en-Laye.
1630	•	The Massachusetts Bay Company establishes a Puritan colony for England.
1633	•	Lord Baltimore founds Maryland for England.
	•	The first Puritan settlers arrive in Connecticut.
1635	•	Massachusetts Bay Colony exile Roger Williams founds Providence Plantation.
1636–37	•	The Pequot War ravages the Indians of Connecticut.
1638	•	Puritans from Massachusetts Bay Colony found New Haven Colony.
	•	The Swedish settle Delaware. In 1655 the Dutch take over.
1640s–1680s	•	The Iroquois wage war on their Huron, Mohican, Susquehannock, and French rivals in the fur trade. The Huron are wiped out and replaced by the Ottawa as France's main trading partner.

1642	•	The French found Montreal.
1643–47	•	The Dutch crush the Wappinger Confederacy.
1644	•	The Tidewater tribes initiate another rebellion, which leads to their defeat.
1653	•	The Dutch surrender their trading post on the Connecticut River to England.
1654	•	England takes Acadia from France; it is returned in 1667.
1655–64	•	Wars between the Dutch and the Indians along the Hudson River.
1664	•	England takes New Netherland from the Dutch and renames it New York; Fort Orange is renamed Albany.
1669–87	•	René-Robert Cavelier de La Salle explores the Great Lakes and sails down the Mississippi River for France.
1670	•	England charters the Hudson's Bay Company.
1675–76	•	King Philip's War ends in the defeat of New England's Indians.
1676	•	Nathaniel Bacon defeats Nanticoke and Susquehannock Indians in the Virginia Piedmont.
1680	•	Popé leads the Great Pueblo Revolt of 1680, forcing the Spanish out of the Southwest.
1680s–1690s	•	French efforts to crush the Iroquois fail.
1682	•	Quaker leader William Penn founds Philadelphia and signs a treaty with the leaders of the Delaware Confederacy, establishing the colony of Pennsylvania.
1689	•	Spain establishes the first Catholic mission in Texas and begins the reconquest of the Pueblo Indians.
1689–97	•	King William's War. The English take Port Royal in 1690 but return it in the 1697 Treaty of Ryswick.
1699–75	•	Pierre Le Moyne d'Iberville explores the Mississippi River delta for France.

1702–13	•	Queen Anne's War. The English win Acadia.
1711–13	•	The Tuscarora War in North Carolina. Most of the tribe is wiped out.
1713	•	The French build a fortress at Louisbourg on Île-Royale (Cape Breton Island).
1715–28	•	Yamasee Indians fight colonists in South Carolina.
1718	•	Jean-Baptiste Le Moyne, sieur de Bienville, founds New Orleans.
1720–52	•	The French ally with the Choctaw and fight an ongoing war with the Chickasaw along the lower Mississippi River.
1722	•	The surviving Tuscarora join the Iroquois League of Five Nations.
1729	•	The French defeat the Natchez Indians in Louisiana.
1733	•	James Oglethorpe founds the settlement of Savannah, Georgia.
1740–50	•	Civil war among the Choctaw.
1741	•	Vitus Bering, a Dane, sails from Russia to Alaska.
1744–48	•	King George's War.
1749	•	The British found Halifax, Nova Scotia and start harassing the French Acadians.
1754–63	•	The French and Indian War. The English capture Quebec City and Montreal in 1760. In the Treaty of Paris, France cedes New France to England and Louisiana to Spain.
1758	•	The English initiate the Acadian Expulsion. More than 6,000 Acadians are deported to France; some flee to Louisiana.
1760–61	•	Carolina colonists wage war with the Cherokee.
1763	•	England's King George III issues a proclamation prohibiting white settlement west of the Appalachian Mountains. Pontiac's Rebellion of the Ottawa around the Great Lakes protests white violations.

1768–69 • A Spanish colonizing expedition arrives in California. Fray Junípero Serra founds San Diego.

1770s • New Spain reaches its greatest extent.

1774 • Settlers in Virginia fight the Shawnee Indians.

1775 • Richard Henderson buys portions of present-day Kentucky and Tennessee from the Cherokee.

1775–81 • The American Revolution. Most Indians side with the British against the rebellious American colonists. The American victory is formalized in the 1783 Treaty of Paris.

1782–86 • British loyalists migrate from the United States to British North America.

1783 • Russians found their first permanent settlement in North America, on Kodiak Island, Alaska.

1784 • The North West Company of Montreal starts competing with the Hudson's Bay Company for the Canadian fur trade.

1787 • The United States Congress passes the Northwest Ordinance and drafts the Constitution.

1790 • Spain signs the Nootka Convention, ceding the Pacific Northwest to Britain and the United States.

1790–95 • Little Turtle's War in the Northwest Territory ends in the Treaty of Fort Greenville.

1794 • The United States and Canada sign the Jay Treaty, allowing Mohawk traders to travel freely between British North America and the United States.

1795 • The Unites States and Spain sign Pinckney's Treaty.

1800 • Spain returns Louisiana to France.

1803 • The United States makes the Louisiana Purchase from France.

1803–6 • Meriwether Lewis and William Clark explore the Louisiana Purchase.

1806–22	•	The United States War Department operates trading factories in Indian country.
1811	•	Tecumseh's Rebellion is crushed at the Battle of Tippecanoe.
1812	•	Scottish Highlanders establish Fort Douglas in Assiniboia, Canada.
1812–14	•	The War of 1812 between Britain and the United States ends in the Treaty of Ghent, signed in 1815.
1813–14	•	American forces defeat the Creek in the Southeast.
1815–17	•	Fighting between Métis and whites in Assiniboia ends with the Selkirk Treaty.
1817–18	•	The First Seminole War in Florida.
1819	•	Spain cedes Florida to the United States.
1820	•	The United States Congress passes the Missouri Compromise, admitting Missouri as a slave state and Maine as a free state.
1821	•	The Hudson's Bay and North West companies merge.
	•	Mexico gains its independence from Spain.
1825	•	The United States Congress sets aside Indian Country.
1827	•	Winnebago Indians resist white advancement into Wisconsin.
1830	•	The United States Congress passes the Indian Removal Act.
1831–39	•	The Unites States Army forces the "Five Civilized Tribes" from the Southeast to Indian Country. In 1838–39 the Cherokee endure the Trail of Tears.
1832	•	In the Black Hawk War, the Sauk and Fox Indians resist white settlement in Illinois and Wisconsin.
1836	•	The Lone Star Republic of Texas declares its independence from Mexico.
1840	•	Overtrapping virtually ends the North American fur trade.

1841–42 • Americans John Charles Frémont and Kit Carson explore Oregon Country. White settlers start pouring west along the Oregon Trail.

1842 • The Webster-Ashburton Treaty sets the border between Maine and British North America.

1845 • The United States annexes Texas, igniting the Mexican War in 1846.

1846 • The Oregon Boundary Treaty sets the western United States–British North America boundary at the 49th parallel.

1847 • The Mormon republic of Deseret is founded near the Great Salt Lake of Utah.

1848 • Britain agrees to grant internal self-rule to the provinces of British North America.

• The United States wins the Mexican War and gains the Southwest and California north of the Gila River.

1849 • The Courthouse Rebellion by the Métis of Canada.

• The United States Department of Interior takes over the Bureau of Indian Affairs from the War Department.

• The discovery of gold in California starts a gold rush.

1850 • The United States Congress passes the Compromise of 1850, admitting California as a free state.

1850s– • Numerous wars between whites and Indians in the
1870s American Northwest.

1853 • The United States makes the Gadsden Purchase, acquiring from Mexico a strip of land south of the Gila River.

1854 • The United States Congress passes the Kansas-Nebraska Act, opening a large portion of Indian Territory to white settlement.

1855–58 • The Third Seminole Uprising in Florida.

1858 • Gold rushes start in British Columbia, Colorado, and Nevada.

1860	•	The Canadian provinces gain control of Indian affairs.
1861–65	•	The Civil War in the United States.
1861–86	•	The Apache Uprising in the American Southwest. Years of sporadic fighting end with the surrender of Geronimo.
1862	•	The United States Congress passes the Homestead Act, granting 160-acre farms to white settlers in Kansas and Nebraska.
1863–66	•	The Navajo War in New Mexico.
1864	•	Canadian maritime provinces discuss unification at Charlottetown, Prince Edward Island.
	•	The Quebec Conference outlines a plan for forming a confederation of Canadian provinces.
	•	Indian war breaks out on the Great Plains.
1865–1880s	•	Ranchers drive huge herds of cattle across the plains, overgrazing buffalo pastureland.
1867	•	The British North American Act confederates the provinces of Canada, Nova Scotia, and New Brunswick into the Dominion of Canada and splits the Province of Canada into Ontario and Quebec.
	•	Russia sells Alaska to the United States.
1869	•	The Canadian confederation buys Rupert's Land from the Hudson's Bay Company and renames it the Northwest Territories.
	•	The First Riel Rebellion by the Métis of Canada.
	•	The Transcontinental Railroad, linking the American East and West coasts, is completed.
1871	•	The United States stops recognizing Indian tribes as sovereign nations and signs no further treaties.
	•	Indians are barred from leaving reservations without permission.

- Mass slaughter of American buffalo by white hunters begins.

1872–73 • The Modoc War ends Indian resistance in California.

1873 • The North West Mounted Police (the Mounties) are organized in Canada.

1876–77 • Sioux chiefs Sitting Bull and Crazy Horse assist the Cheyenne in the Sioux War. The war includes the famous Battle of Little Bighorn.

1877 • The Nez Percé War defeats that tribe in the American Northwest.

1881–85 • Construction of the Canadian Pacific Railroad.

1885 • The Second Riel Rebellion by the Métis. The execution of Louis Riel suppresses Indian resistance throughout Canada.

- White hunters wipe out the last great buffalo herd in the United States.

1887 • The United States Congress passes the General Allotment (Dawes Severalty) Act, further reducing Indian Territory.

1889 • The Oklahoma Land Run.

1890 • Attempting to crush the Ghost Dance religious movement among the Plains Indians, American troops kill Sitting Bull and massacre 150 Sioux Indians at Wounded Knee, South Dakota. The Indian Wars end in the United States.

1896–98 • The Klondike Gold Rush to northern Canada and Alaska.

FURTHER READING

NONFICTION

Adams, Alexander B., *Sunlight and Storm: The Great American Plains* (New York: G. P. Putnam's Sons, 1977). A truly fascinating depiction of the events and people of the western conquest.

Boorstin, Daniel J., ed., *An American Primer* (Chicago: University of Chicago Press, 1966). Solid information on the 19th-century expansion of the United States.

Bowman, John S., ed., *The World Almanac of the American West* (New York: World Almanac/Pharos, 1986). Excellent illustrated reference with sidebars, maps, chronologies, and other useful features.

Brebner, J. Bartlett, *Canada*, new ed., rev. and enlarged by Donald C. Masters (Ann Arbor, MI: University of Michigan Press, 1970). A comprehensive history of Canada from prehistory to the 1960s.

Bumsted, J. M., *The Peoples of Canada: A Pre-Confederation History* (Toronto: Oxford University Press, 1992). An up-to-date history of Canada through the early confederation period, with special attention to social and cultural subjects.

Debo, Angie, *A History of the Indians of the United States* (Noman, OK: University of Oklahoma Press, 1970). A readable and sympathetic narrative of the conquest of U.S. Indians, despite some factual inaccuracies.

Dippie, Brian W., *The Vanishing American: White Attitudes and U.S. Indian Policy* (Middletown, CT: Wesleyan University Press, 1982). An unflinching and moving study of the destruction of Native American culture during the white conquest.

Eccles, William J., *The Canadian Frontier, 1534–1760* (New York: Holt, Rhinehart and Winston, 1969). An engaging narrative of Canadian history up through 1760.

Fehrenbacher, Don E., *The Era of Expansion: 1800–1848* (New York: John Wiley & Sons, 1981). A competent examination of the United States' westward growth, with abundant attention to the impact on Native Americans.

Fenton, William N., ed., *Parker on the Iroquois* (Syracuse, NY: Syracuse University Press, 1968). A collection of Arthur C. Parker's definitive history of the Five Nations, with extensive primary source material.

Gabriel, Ralph Henry, *The Lure of the Frontier: A Story of Race Conflict* (New Haven, CT: Yale University Press, 1929). A detailed survey of white advancement across the American West and the Indian wars it provoked.

Goodman, Edward J., *The Explorers of South America* (Norman, OK: University of Oklahoma Press, 1992.) Of interest for its coverage of early Spanish conquest.

Goodman, Paul and Frank Otto Gatell, *The American Colonial Experience: An Essay in National Origins* (New York: Holt, Rhinehart and Winston, 1970). The story of English settlement on the Atlantic seaboard.

Greene, Jack P., ed., *Settlements to Society: 1584–1763*, vol. 1 (New York: McGraw-Hill Book Company, 1966). Writings on the settlement of the English colonies by people who were there.

Hafen, LeRoy R., et. al., *Western America* (Englewood Cliffs, NJ: Prentice-Hall, 1970). A sturdy rendering of the familiar tale.

Harris, Neil, et. al., eds., *American History, 1600 to the Present: Source Readings* (New York: Holt, Rinehart and Winston, 1969). An absorbing collection of primary source material reflecting the history of the United States.

Hawke, David, *Colonial Experience* (Indianapolis, IN: Bobbs-Merrill Company, 1966). A fine summary of English colonization of the future United States.

Heizer, Robert F. and Alan F. Almquist, *The Other Californians* (Berkeley, CA: University of California Press, 1971). A tale of Indian mistreatment by Spain, Mexico, and the United States.

Josephy, Alvin M., *The Indian Heritage of America* (Boston: Houghton Mifflin, 1991). An in-depth look at North and South American Indian cultures, with closing chapters on the impact of white conquest.

Keen, Benjamin, *A History of Latin America* (Boston: Houghton Mifflin Company, 1992.) A well-written text on Spanish conquistadores.

Lamar, Howard R., ed., *The Reader's Encyclopedia of the American West* (New York: Thomas Y. Crowell Company, 1977). An exhaustive and useful reference.

Morgan, Ted, *Wilderness at Dawn: The Settling of the North American Continent* (New York: Simon & Schuster, 1993). With a focus on the territory that became the United States, this volume presents a highly readable and human story of white activity and its repercussions in North America through the 18th century.

Morison, Samuel Eliot, *The European Discovery of America: The Northern Voyages, A.D. 500–1600* (New York: Oxford University Press, 1971). A thorough history of European explorations of the North American coast from the Carolinas to Arctic Canada.

———, *The European Discovery of America: The Southern Voyages, 1492–1616* (New York: Oxford University Press, 1974). A highly detailed account of European explorations of the Caribbean Sea and coastal America from Florida to Cape Horn to California.

Morison, Samuel Eliot, ed., *The Parkman Reader* (Boston: Little, Brown and Company, 1955). Selections from the multivolume *France and England in North America*, written by Francis Parkman in the late 19th century. Covers Canadian history up through 1760.

Osgood, Ernest Staples, *The Day of the Cattleman* (Chicago: University of Chicago Press, 1966). The story of cattle driving across the Great Plains in the late 19th century.

Paul, Rodman W., *California Gold: The Beginning of Mining in the Far West* (Lincoln, NB: University of Nebraska Press, 1967). An introduction to the white hunger for mineral expoitation of North America.

Remini, Robert V., *The Age of Jackson* (Columbia, SC: University of South Carolina Press, 1972). Extensive coverage of American expansion in the Southeast and the Northwest Territories.

Tindall, George Brown, *America: A Narrative History*, vol. 1 and 2 (New York: W. W. Norton & Company, 1988). A highly reliable and accessible general history of the United States.

Waldman, Carl, *Atlas of the North American Indian* (New York: Facts On File, 1985). An overview of all aspects of Native American culture and history, from antiquity to the present. Many useful maps.

Webb, Walter Prescott, *The Great Plains* (Lincoln, NB: University of Nebraska Press, 1959). A history of the white movement onto the Great Plains.

Williams, Eric, *From Columbus to Castro: The History of the Caribbean* (New York: Vintage Books, 1984). Good background on a subject unfamiliar to most North American students.

FICTION

Aridjis, Homer, *1492: The Life and Times of Juan Cabezón of Castile* (New York: Plume, 1992). Spain during the age of expansion.

Cameron, Anne, *Daughters of Copper Woman* (Vancouver, BC: Press Gang Publishers, 1981). A recounting of the ancient myths of the Northwest Coast Indians.

Cather, Willa, *My Ántonia* (New York: Houghton Mifflin, 1988). A portrait of a pioneer woman in Nebraska; one of the truly great works of American literature.

———, *O Pioneers!* (New York: Penguin Books, 1989). A family of Swedish immigrants struggles to make a life on the Nebraska prairies.

————, *Shadows on the Rock* (New York: Vintage Books, 1971). French adventurers and settlers in 18th-century Quebec.

Cooper, James Fenimore, *The Deerslayer* (New York: Penguin, 1987). One of the Leatherstocking Tales depicting northern New York during the French and Indian Wars.

————, *The Last of the Mohicans* (New York: Bantam, 1981). One of the Leatherstocking Tales depicting northern New York during the French and Indian Wars.

————, *The Pathfinder* (New York: Signet, 1980). One of the Leatherstocking Tales depicting northern New York during the French and Indian Wars.

————, *The Pioneers* (New York: Bantam, 1993). One of the Leatherstocking Tales depicting northern New York during the French and Indian Wars.

————, *The Prairie* (New York: Penguin, 1989). One of the Leatherstocking Tales, this one following the progress of a wagon train across the frontier.

Dillard, Annie, *The Living* (New York: HarperPerennial, 1992). White settlers in the Pacific Northwest in the late 19th century.

Doctorow, E. L., *Welcome to Hard Times* (New York: Fawcett Crest, 1960). Life in a fictional town on the Dakota frontier.

Edmonds, Walter D., *Drums Along the Mohawk* (New York: Bantam, 1992). White settlers during the American Revolution.

Fergus, Charles, *Shadow Catcher* (New York: Soho Press, 1991). Indians endeavor to cope with the impact of white expansion.

Fuentes, Carlos, *Terra Nostra* (New York: Farrar, Strauss & Giroux, 1976). Spanish explorers and conquistadores in the New World.

Guthrie, A. B., *The Big Sky* (New York: Houghton Mifflin, 1992). A beautiful rendering of life on the American frontier.

————, *The Way West* (New York: Houghton Mifflin, 1993). A follow-up to *The Big Sky* tracing the passage of pioneers along the Oregon Trail.

Hawthorne, Nathaniel, *The Scarlet Letter* (New York: Vintage Books, 1990). The life ways of Puritan colonists in New England.

Horgan, Paul, *A Distant Trumpet* (Boston: David R. Godine, 1991). Indian-white conflicts in the American Southwest after the Civil War.

Le Sueur, Meridel, *North Star Country* (Lincoln, NB: University of Nebraska Press, 1984). Pioneer farmers in the Midwest.

Magnusson, Magnus and Hermann Palsson, translators, *The Vinland Sagas: The Norse Discovery of America* (New York: Penguin, 1990). The original Viking legends of the first European voyages to the New World.

Michener, James, *Alaska* (New York: Fawcett Crest, 1988). A saga of Alaska from prehistory to modern times.

————, *Centennial* (New York: Fawcett Crest, 1974). A saga of Colorado from prehistory to modern times.

————, *Chesapeake* (New York: Fawcett Crest, 1978). A saga of the Chesapeake Bay region from prehistory to modern times.

————, *Texas* (New York: Fawcett Crest, 1985). A saga of Texas from prehistory to modern times.

Norris, Frank, *The Octopus* (New York: Penguin, 1991). White competition for land in the American West, pitting farmers against railroad companies.

Rölvaag, O. E., *Giants in the Earth* (New York: HarperPerennial, 1991). Norwegian immigrants on the Dakota prairie meet the challenge of carving a living from the land.

Seidman, Robert J., *One Smart Indian* (Woodstock, NY: Overlook Press, 1979). The Cheyenne Indians face destruction at the hands of the United States Army.

Twain, Mark, *Roughing It* (New York: Signet, 1980). A humorous look at the picturesque characters of the Wild West.

INDEX

Boldface numbers indicate major topics.
Italic numbers indicate illustrations.
Numbers followed by *"m"* indicate maps.

coureurs de bois (runners of the woods) 43, 51
Courthouse Rebellion (1849) 102, 134
cowtowns 120
crafts *See* basketry; woodworking
Crazy Horse (Sioux chief) 121, 136
Cree Indians 6, 97, 105
Creek Indians
  agricultural economy 12
  land given up by 90
  participation in imperial wars 80, 81
  removal from lands 113, 114, 133
  wars and expeditions against 36, 133
crops *See specific types* (*e.g.,* tobacco)
cross-staff (nautical instrument) 23
Crow Indians 13
Crusades 24–25
Cuba 32
Custer, George A. 121

Dakota Territory *117*
Dare, Virginia 59
Dawes Severalty Act (General Allotment Act) (1887) 121, 136
Declaration of Independence (1776) 88
deer 12
Deganawida (Huron mystic) 11
Delaware (state) 65, 129
Delaware Confederacy 66, 130
Delaware Indians 8, 82, 83, 109
Delaware Prophet, the (Neolin) 85
de Monts, Pierre du Gua, sieur 46
Deseret (Mormon republic) 117, 134
de Soto, Hernando 34, 35–36, 128
Detroit (English fort) 86
d'Iberville, Pierre Le Moyne, sieur 55, 79, 130
diptheria 35
diseases
  bubonic plague 35
  cholera 35, 119
  common cold 45
  diptheria 35
  malaria 61
  measles 17, 35, 126
  scarlet fever 35
  smallpox 17, 35, 49, 64, 103, 126
  syphilis 126
  typhus 17, 35, 126
dogs 13
dogsleds 126
Donnacona (Iroquois chief) 45
Drake, Francis *41,* 41–42, 57, 128
"drift voyages" 20

Duquesne, Ange de Menneville, marquis de 82
Durham, John George Lambton, the earl of 101
Dutch East India Company 64, 128
Dutch West India Company 64

El Dorado (fabled land of wealth) 33, 37
Elizabeth I, Queen (England) 41, 42, 58
elk 6
England 25, 47, 49, 50, **57–73,** 130, 131
  See also specific events (*e.g.,* American Revolution); *people* (*e.g.,* George III, King)
English Canada Company 73
English colonies **57–73**
epidemics 50, 68, 94, 119 *See also specific diseases* (*e.g.,* smallpox)
Eriksson, Leif 21, 127
Estevanico (Spanish explorer) 37, 128
Europe **19–26,** 76–77*m See also specific countries* (*e.g.,* France)
Everglades (Florida) 114, 115
expeditions and exploration 19–42, 44–49, 52, 59, 71, 90–91, 97 *See also* conquistadores; *specific explorers* (*e.g.,* Champlain)

Fallen Timbers (1794) 109
felt hats 46
Ferdinand, King (Spain) 26, 32, 34
Ferrelo, Bartolomé 40
fishing 5, 6, 12, 14, 59, 71, 72 *See also specific fish* (*e.g.,* salmon)
"Five Civilized Tribes" (Cherokee, Choctaw, Creek, Chickasaw, and Seminole) 113, 133
Five Nations, League of *See* League of Five Nations
Florida **33–36,** 80–81, 127, 128, 133 *See also* Seminole Indians
Forbes, John 84
Fort Caroline 35, 43
Fort Christina 65
Fort Douglas 97, 98, 133
Fort Duquesne 83, 84
Fort Garry 99
Fort Greenville, Treaty of (1795) 109, 132
Fort Langley 99
Fort Laramie 120
Fort Orange 64, 129, 130
Fort Pitt 84, 87, 98
Fort Rosalie 55
Fort St. Frederick 81, 84
Fort William 98
"Fountain of Youth" 34

Nebraska 120, 134, 135
Neolin (the Delaware Prophet) (Delaware spiritual leader) 85
Netherlands 25, 64–65, 79, 129–130
Nevada 117, 134
New Amsterdam **64–65,** 129
New Brunswick (Canada) 86, 103, 135
New Ebenezer (Georgia) 64
New England **66–71** *See also specific places (e.g., Massachusetts)*
New England Company 67
Newfoundland (Canada) 21, 60, 72, *72,* 103, 106, 127, 128
New France **43–56**
New Hampshire 67, 81, 87
New Haven Colony 70, 129
New Jersey 65
New Mexico 16, 91, 119, 129, 135
New Orleans (Louisiana) 44, 55, 131
New Spain **31–42**
New York 65, 81, 87, 130
New York Harbor 64, 128
Nez Percé Indians 14, 115–116
Nez Percé War (1877) 136
Niantic Indians 68
Niña (ship) 26
Nipissing Indians 82
Nootka Convention (1790) 97, 132
Norse (Vikings) 21, 127
North Carolina 63, 88, 114, 131 *See also* Roanoke Island
North Dakota 122
North Virginia Company of Plymouth 58, 60
North West Company 93, 97, 98, 132, 133
North West Mounted Police *See* Mounties
Northwest Ordinance (1787) 90, 132
Northwest Passage 44, 57, 59, 71
Northwest Territories 97, 103, 106, 109–110, 135
Nova Scotia 72, 86, 103, 129, 131, 135 *See also* Acadia; Port Royal
nuts 12, 14, 126

oats 126
Oglethorpe, James 63, 131
Ohio 109, 112
Ohio Company of Virginia 82
Ohio Valley 10, 82, 87, 90, 127
Ojibwa (Chippewa) Indians 8, 49, 82, 109, 110
Oklahoma 108, 122
Oklahoma Land Run (1889) 121–122, 136
Omaha Indians 12
Oñate, Juan de 39, 128
Oneida Indians 10, 11, 79, 89, 128

Onondaga Indians 10, 11, 48, 79, 89, 128
Ontario (Canada) 96, 101, 103, 135
Opechancanough (Tidewater Indian leader) 62
Oregon Boundary Treaty (1846) 102, 134
Oregon Country 99, 115, 134
Oregon Trail 115, 134
Osage Indians 12
Ottawa Indians 49, 50, 79, 82, 109, 131
otters 46

Pacific Northwest **6–8** *See also specific places (e.g., Oregon Country)*
Paiute Indians 14
Paiute War (1860) 117
Pamlico Indians 8
Pamukey Indians 62–63
Papineau, Louis-Joseph 100
Paris, Treaty of (1763) 86, 131
Paris, Treaty of (1783) 89, 132
Patuxet Indians 61, 67
Paul I, Czar (Russia) 118
Pawnee Indians 12
peanuts 126
pemmican 98
Penn, William 65, 66, 130
Pennsylvania 65, 66, 90, 130 *See also* Philadelphia
Penobscot Indians 8
Pepperell, William 81
peppers 126
Pequot Indians 8, 68
Pequot War (1636–37) 68–69, 129
Peralta, Pedro de 39
Philadelphia (Pennsylvania) 66, 130
Phipps, William 79
pigs 126
Pilgrims 66–67, 129
Pinckney's Treaty (1795) 112, 132
Pinta (ship) 26
piracy 33
Pitt, William 84
Pizarro, Francisco 32
Plains *See* Great Plains
Plains Indians 40, 119–122, *122,* 136
Plains of Abraham, Battle of the (1760) 85
Plateau **13, 14**
Plymouth Colony 67, 129
Polo, Marco 24
Ponce de León, Juan 34, 127
Pontiac (Ottawa chief) 85, 86
Pontiac's Rebellion (1763) 131
Popé (Pueblo Indian leader) 39, 40, 130
Port Royal (Nova Scotia) 46–47, 73
Portugal 23, 25, 26, 28

potatoes 4, 59, 126
Potawatomi Indians 82, 109, 110, 111
potlatch 7–8
Poundmaker (Cree chief) 105
Poutrincourt, Charles de Biencourt de 47
Poutrincourt, Jean de Biencourt de 47
Powhatan *See* Wahunsonacock
Powhatan Confederacy 62
Powhatan Indians 8, 129
Prince Edward Island (Canada) 80, 86, 103
Prophet (Shawnee visionary) 110
Protestants 25, 65, 86, 103 *See also* Puritans; Reformation
Providence Plantation 68, 129
Pueblo Indians 16, 38–40, 119, 128, 130
Puerto Rico 32
Puritans 66–71, 129

quadrant (nautical instrument) 23
Quakers 66
Quebec (Canada) 44, 48–49, 85, 96, 101, 135
Quebec Act (1774) 86
Quebec City (Quebec, Canada) 45, 47, 85, 85
Quebec Conference (1864) 103, 135
Queen Anne's War (1702–13) 79, 131

rabbits 14
railroads
    Canadian Pacific 104, 136
    Central Pacific 120
    Transcontinental 120, 135
    Union Pacific 120
Raleigh, Walter 58, 59, 128
Rebellions of 1837 100
Red Sticks *See* Upper Creek Indians
Reformation 19, 25
"Regulators" 87
Renaissance 19, 22, 25
reptiles 14
reservations 109, 116, 120, 121, 135
Revere, Paul 88
Rhode Island Plantation 68
Ribaut, Jean 35, 43
rice 8, 63, 126
Riel, Louis (Courthouse Rebellion leader) 102
Riel, Louis (Riel Rebellions leader) 103–105, *105*, 136
Riel Rebellion, First (1869) 103, 135
Riel Rebellion, Second (1885) 104, 136
Roanoke Island (North Carolina) 59–60, 128
Roberval, sieur de 46

Rochambeau, Jean-Baptiste-Donatien de Vimeur, comte de 89
rodents 14
Roman Catholics
    dissidents from England 65
    European conflicts over religion 24–25
    French Catholics in Canada 80, 86, 103
    missions and missionaries 36, 40, 50, 90, 116, 130
Ross, Alexander 51
Royal Proclamation of 1763 86, 88
Rupert's Land 97–99, 102
Russia 84, 90, 115, 118, 132, 135
Russian American Company 118
Ryswyck, Treaty of (1697) 79, 130

Saguenay (legendary land of wealth) 45, 46
sailing ships 23
St. Augustine (Florida) 35
St. Brendan (Irish friar) 20
Saint Étienne de la Tour, Charles de 47
Saint Étienne de la Tour, Claude de 47
Saint-Germain-en-Laye, Treaty of (1632) 49, 73, 129
salmon 7, 14
Samoset (Wampanoag Indian) 67
Sampson, Deborah 88
San Antonio (Texas) 91
San Diego (California) 91, 132
Santa Anna, Antonio López de 119
Santa Fe (New Mexico) 129
Santa Fe Trail 117
Santa Maria (ship) 27, 28
Saskatchewan (Canada) 97, 105
Sauk Indians 82, 109, 111, 133
Saunders, Charles 85
Savannah (Georgia) 64, 131
Sawyer, Guillaume 102
scarlet fever 35
seals 5, 72
sea otters 90, 126
sea voyages 20–21, 23, 26–29 *See also* Northwest Passage
Second Continental Congress 87
secret societies 7, 13
seigneurial system 51–52
Selkirk, Thomas Douglas, earl of 97–99
Selkirk Treaty (1817) 99, 133
Seminole Indians 12, 113, 114, 115, 133
Seminole War, First (1817–18) 113, 133
Seminole War, Second (1835–42) 114
Seminole War, Third (1855–58) 114, 134
Semple, Robert 98
Seneca Indians 10, 11, 20, 82, 89, 128
Serra, Junípero 91, 132

EUROPEAN CONQUEST OF NORTH AMERICA